CHARLOTTE
CHURCH

HELL'S ANGEL

CHARLOTTE CHURCH

HELL'S ANGEL

STEVE JOHNSON
WITH NEIL SIMPSON

JOHN BLAKE

Published by John Blake Publishing Ltd,
3, Bramber Court, 2 Bramber Road,
London W14 9PB, England

www.blake.co.uk

First published in paperback in 2005

ISBN 1 84454 177 0

British Library Cataloguing-in-Publication Data:

A catalogue record for this book is available from the British Library.

Design by www.envydesign.co.uk

Printed in Great Britain by Creative Print & Design (Wales)

1 3 5 7 9 10 8 6 4 2

Papers used by John Blake Publishing are natural, recyclable products made
from wood grown in sustainable forests. The manufacturing processes conform to
the environmental regulations of the country of origin.

All pictures © Rex Features, except: p5 bottom, p8 Empics and p5 top,
author collection.

CONTENTS

INTRODUCTION
THE WRONG LABELS

Charlotte Church was first labelled when she was just 11 years old. Her record company said she had the voice of an angel – and the public wanted her to live like one for the rest of her life.

Charlotte, of course, had other ideas. When I first met her she was 15 and was already desperate to shake off the 'angel' tag. By the time we moved in together, less than a year later she had pretty much succeeded and today you only need open a newspaper to see how completely she has changed her image.

She's a complex character and it's always frustrated me that her public hasn't been allowed to see her as I have. I've always wanted people to know the wonderful Charlotte I loved, not the one-dimensional character the media would like her to be.

But I've never been able to get my own side of our love story across, the truth of our devotion for one another. I was landed with a label as soon as the press found out that I was dating Charlotte. I was called the 'bad boy', the 'bit of rough' and the 'teenage tearaway' who was leading Charlotte astray and dragging the angel down into the gutter.

I am writing this book because my label has stuck and I want to clear up all the lies and exaggerations that have been printed about Charlotte and me over the years. Very few people really know who Charlotte really is, what drives her forward and the depth of our love for one another. People don't know about the bad times that have shaped her or the pressure she has always been under. And people certainly don't know what I'm really like. This is my chance to put the record straight on all counts.

Charlotte and I were just teenagers when we met. Like every other teenager in the world, we wanted to be cool. We wanted to be edgy, to look good, to wear the right clothes, hang out with the right people and go to the right places. We wanted to impress our mates, stand out from the crowd and have a bit of fun because everyone told us that we were only young once. My extra baggage was that I also wanted to look hard. I was a Computer Studies student with a makeshift music studio in my mum's back bedroom. I was as shy as hell and deep down I knew I could be labelled a nerd. So, as a teenager from an inner-city street, looking cool and acting hard meant more to me than most.

Because of all that I didn't really mind being labelled

a 'bad boy' when I first met and fell in love with Charlotte Church. It didn't bother me how often the papers said I came from 'a broken home in the wrong part of town' or if they said I was Charlotte's 'bit of rough'. I never once recognised myself from what was written about me in the papers, so I didn't think any of those descriptions mattered. I was 17 and I was having my first real love affair so I didn't really care about what anyone else thought of me.

But I started to care soon enough.

Looking back I still can't believe that everything went so wrong with me and Charlotte. All I ever really wanted was to be with that great girl who first came round to my dad's house with her mates, telling dirty jokes, laughing, flirting and catching my eye. I wanted to be with the girl who liked my kind of music, watched my kind of films, shared my view of the world and laughed alongside me at everyone in it. That girl was the Charlotte Church I first knew – the one I first kissed, fell in love, travelled and ultimately lived with. She was the one I reckon I would still love today, if we had been ordinary teenagers, left to make a go of their lives in private without other people trying to interfere and change us. And if we hadn't had two families who were pretty much hostile to each other from the start.

But my girlfriend was a 'teenage multi-millionaire' from a 'luxury mansion' in a posh suburb. Meanwhile, I was 'the penniless student from a crime-torn council estate'. Maybe I should have realised that this would be an irresistible combination for reporters desperate to whip up some celebrity gossip and sell some newspapers.

Charlotte and I didn't just have to put up with being attacked and laughed at by the newspapers. There was always a third person in our relationship as well – just as I think there always will be in every relationship that Charlotte ever has. That extra person is her mother, Maria, the woman who has been called the original Welsh dragon.

As I write this book Charlotte and Maria seem to be back on track. They're photographed together all the time and she's giving Charlotte's latest relationship all her support. That's not the Maria I remember, and I'm not sure that she won't turn back into the old Maria before long – the one who made Charlotte cry so long and so hard when she was 16 and we were both living with my dad.

I want people to know how great Charlotte was when I fell in love with her. I want to show how many pressures she has had to put up with in her life, and how she has changed because of them. And I want to warn others just how easy it is to get burned when you're in the public eye.

When I first met Charlotte she was one of the most media-savvy teenagers in the country. I wasn't. I read the sport and the gossip in the tabloids and I laughed with my mates about some of the stories. But I had no idea how newspapers worked or just how many of those stories were outright lies. I certainly didn't know just how hard it can be to shake off those lies once they're in print. Today, I think I know as much as Charlotte and her family about how the media works. Like them I've seen the games that reporters play, how they push and push for a reaction and can twist almost any words to fit the stories they've already written in their heads. I have also seen how certain people can plant stories and set up situations to suit their own needs and goals – and how one little white lie can have repercussions that can change the course of someone's life.

'The media interest was really hard for Steve and I was sorry that I didn't have a chance to warn him,' Charlotte said on television when Michael Parkinson asked how we had coped with all the interest when our relationship first became public property. It was typically sweet of her to say that, but even if she had I was so in love with her by then that I probably wouldn't have taken any notice.

Reporters still ring me or approach me to talk about Charlotte. At least now, by reading this book, they will know the truth about this passionate girl and the relationship we had that literally went around the world.

I also want this book to be my way of thanking all the people who have supported and helped me over the years. My mum, my dad, my sisters and all of my family are top of the list. Then there are neighbours, friends, the teachers and my headmistress at school, plus all the staff at my old college and at Intech, all of whom have given me so much. I may not always show it, but I appreciate it and I know how much all this is really worth.

Loving Charlotte Church was brilliant because for so long she was brilliant. But dealing with the media and all the people around her turned everything into a nightmare. Like I say, I never recognised the Steve Johnson that the papers wrote about in the one I saw in the mirror. But by the end of the relationship, I didn't really recognise the Charlotte Church that I first fell in love with in the one I was living with, either. The forces that pulled us apart were just too much – I wouldn't wish that kind of pressure on anyone. This is how it all happened and where it all went wrong.

CHAPTER ONE

IT'S VEGAS, BABY

Imagine holding your girlfriend's hand when you fly first class into Las Vegas. Imagine knowing that she's talented, professional and about to give a knock-out performance to 7,000 fans in the entertainment capital of the world. Knowing that she could have chosen almost anyone to sit next to on that plane – her mother, her stepfather, her manager, one of her best friends or anyone in her entourage. But she picked you instead.

When you are 18 and in love, it's hard to think of any better position to be in.

It was April 2003 and Charlotte and I had been dating for 14 months and pretty much living together full-time for 10 of them. And we had been trashed and pulled apart by the media for what seemed like a lifetime.

'We're going to be fine, don't worry,' I told Charlotte again and again as our plane got ready to land. Despite all the travelling she had done in her life, Charlotte was still terrified of takeoffs and landings, and she gripped my hand even tighter across the big, first-class seats as we headed down towards the runway in the desert. Once we were safely on the ground I could hardly believe what we could see. The amazing thing about Las Vegas is that all those huge hotels that you see in pictures are actually lined up right alongside the airport. So from the plane's windows we could see the huge black glass pyramid of the Luxor. The replica Eiffel Tower outside the hotel designed to look like Paris. And all the other lights and madness that make up the other vast hotels and resorts in the centre of town.

Charlotte, suddenly excited again, wanted me to see absolutely everything.

Unlike me she'd been to Las Vegas before and she loved it. The most recent time had been just after September 11 in 2001, when she had taken part in a charity concert organised by Andre Agassi. I had seen some of the reviews in the local papers – one of which said she'd stolen the show from the likes of Stevie Wonder and Elton John – and she'd also spent time with Robin Williams and Agassi himself.

As usual, I found myself worrying whether my company could match that of the stars Charlotte had hung out with. But as we got off our plane and into the mandatory big black limo that would take us to the Strip, I started to relax. This place is cool. Very, very cool. How can anyone not have fun in a town like this? Especially two young lovers having the biggest adventure of their lives.

We were treated like royalty when we first rocked up at the five-star Aladdin Hotel and Resort where Charlotte was performing in the big one-off concert that week. The hotel was brand new, and is bang in the middle of the Strip, just down from Caesar's Palace and opposite the Bellagio where they set most of *Ocean's Eleven*. The hotel manager shook us by the hand to welcome us to our suite – one of the penthouses, of course. And, of course, it was huge and totally over-the-top.

'I'll race you!'

Charlotte and I started running around this lavish suite like a pair of little kids, laughing away. We dashed from room to room, window to window, looking out at the fantastic views of the Strip and the mountains. We couldn't believe the size and the luxury of the bathroom. Or the sheer size of the whole place. You could probably have fitted my dad's whole house in that single suite – or the traditional terraced house where Charlotte herself had been born, for that matter. It was impossible not to think about how far we had travelled in life to get to this point.

But when we flopped down on one of the vast beds and opened a couple of cans of drink, we soon calmed down. Both of us had different reactions to this kind of crazy luxury, so there were always other feelings just below the surface. Charlotte – the 17-year-old who had sung at the White House and in front of the Queen – was getting pretty bored by this kind of stuff.

She'd seen luxury before, and the girl who was always equally happy to slob out on my dad's sofa with a takeaway pizza was able to put it all in perspective. I could never stop myself from thinking about who was paying for all this – and what people would say about me being there.

I had been called a gold-digger ever since Charlotte and I had first started going out with each other some 14 months earlier. I'd also been called a leech, a parasite, a sponger and worse. People said I was only with Charlotte for her money. It was like that line from *Mrs Merton* when she was interviewing Debbie McGee: 'So, Debbie, what was it that first attracted you to millionaire Paul Daniels?'

I knew that some people – including Charlotte's family – thought I was only after her cash. More of this later, but for now all I will say is, what cash? Charlotte was on an allowance when we met – I had more cash in my pockets each week than she did, especially when I got a good DJ gig. And trips like this weren't holidays that had been saved up for – they were business trips, paid for by Charlotte's promoters, by the sponsors, record companies or television stations. I wasn't taking anyone's money for being there – certainly not Charlotte's, like most people tried to suggest.

But when I looked at the huge arrangements of fresh flowers in this Vegas room and thought back to the limo that had brought us here, I knew that if I wasn't exactly a fish out of water then that is how I would be treated in the media. Once again they would say I was ligging on the back of my hard-working, high-earning girlfriend.

But what the reporters didn't know was that Charlotte and I had a secret agreement. We had talked about all the glitz and the glamour of her life often enough, and we both knew we could take it or leave it. We would have been just as happy in some dodgy Las Vegas motel, in some flea-bitten, no-star room like in some American road movie. Because both Charlotte and I are very different to our public images.

At that point people always seemed to see Charlotte as a solid-gold, old-fashioned star. She went to premieres, sang for presidents, looked a million dollars on red carpets and big stages and was absolutely at home living the high life. But I knew that she treated it all like a joke and I swear she was telling the truth when she told me she could give it all up and live an ordinary life. I think she has proved that by staying in Cardiff where her friends and family are, rather than heading off to London or America. Two years on from that Vegas trip, it's obvious that Charlotte and I will never share that low-rent motel room, but I wouldn't be surprised if we don't both stay in places like that with other partners. It's a big part of who we are, and it was one of the reasons why I fell in love with Charlotte in the first place.

'Charlotte – look over there. It's you!'

'Oh, my God! I look like a pixie or an air stewardess! Why did I pick that hat?'

We were out on the Strip, looking up at Charlotte's face plastered across some massive billboards advertising her first ever solo concert in the city. There was also a crystal-clear television screen the size of a double-decker bus outside the hotel, playing footage of Charlotte in concert back in Cardiff. So a quiet life of anonymity was hardly an option and, as usual, there were queues of people she had to meet or who wanted to see her before we could relax. Being with Charlotte Church when she was working pretty much meant never being alone. She was other people's investment, other people's product, and they all wanted a piece of her.

'Can you sign some of these programmes, Charlotte? We can give them to the fans.' Her PRs needed some work done and Charlotte, to her credit, was always up for this part of her job. Her mum Maria, not me, had been with her on that awful trip to America the previous December when Charlotte had been accused of slagging off and refusing to meet fans and disabled people at the end of one concert. There were awful newspaper articles in Britain, laying into her for being insensitive, cruel and full of herself, but I never believed it had been anything but a misunderstanding. Yes, Charlotte got tired and stressed when she was working – who wouldn't? But she was always ready to give something back to the fans and the reports of a diva-ish Charlotte yelling things like, 'Fuck this! I never agreed to no meet-and-greet. Hello?' just didn't ring true.

6

Anyway, in Las Vegas Charlotte was happy to talk to the local press and TV stations, to schmooze the senior hotel and casino staff. She was happy to give some time to her PR people, sign this huge new pile of publicity photos and programmes for fans and hit the rehearsal rooms for her big show.

The arena where she was performing in the Aladdin was huge. Vegas doesn't do anything on a small scale, so everything from the equipment to the acoustics was state-of-the-art. They needed to be. Fans were paying top dollar for their tickets, so Charlotte had to give value for money. As if this wouldn't make you nervous enough, Charlotte had extra worries about the material she was going to perform. It was going to be the first time she had sung some of the songs in public. I knew that sometimes in rehearsals she could forget words she had sung a hundred times before in private, and how she worried about following the music and getting all her cues right during the performance itself.

The first rehearsals went well, though, and were watched by a vast team of production and backing staff who all thought the teenager from South Wales was a marvel. As far as many Americans were concerned Wales was pretty cool at that moment, because Catherine Zeta Jones never stopped talking about it from her new home in Hollywood. So we got to coast along on all that good will as well.

After that Charlotte and I had some free time for fun, but because of our ages the two things we couldn't do were drink or gamble. Still, while I'd been waiting for Charlotte to finish a business meeting on our first day, one of the hotel's managers, slightly embarrassed, had told me all about the city's long history of double standards over everything from sex and age to race. In the 1940s and 1950s, for example, the big hotel owners had been happy to cash in and have the likes of Sammy Davis Jr, Nat King Cole and Louis Armstrong performing on their main stages. But because they were black the hotel owners were not so willing to roll out the red carpet for them when the shows were over. I heard the story about one hotel guest who had demanded the hotel pool be drained and refilled after black singer and actress Dorothy Dandridge had just dipped her toe in it for a dare. Then there was the story that chambermaids had been told to burn Dinah Washington's sheets every morning – because heaven forbid that any white guest should sleep on cotton that had once touched a black body.

As a mixed-race man, these stories took on a very personal meaning, so suddenly it didn't seem to matter so much that the hotel could pay a teenager huge sums to sing in its halls but wouldn't let her drink or gamble alongside the other guests afterwards. What we could do was see some of the big shows that rivalled the one Charlotte was giving at the weekend. We pored over the listings magazines and asked the hotel staff which they recommended. Then we picked Cirque du Soleil, the colourful, circus-like acrobatic show that had won rave reviews. Charlotte got the star treatment from the start – the theatre manager was there to greet us and took us for a fantastic meal before we headed to our seats.

'Oh, my God!'

'Oh, my God!'

I think that was pretty much all Charlotte and I kept repeating to each other throughout the show as the cast did their stuff – and if you've ever seen the show you'll know why we were open-mouthed.

'Bloody hell! I hope they're not expecting the same sort of thing from me,' Charlotte whispered as another extraordinary balancing act unfolded in front of us. 'It's hard enough just singing and walking at the same time, let alone doing any of that.'

The next day we had another big outing. Charlotte wanted to hit the shops and there were plenty to choose from. I hadn't realised how many hidden, air-conditioned shopping malls there were in a city that I thought would just be full of slot machines, blackjack and roulette tables. The Aladdin, where we were staying, likes to claim it has a mile of shops running around its vast casino. So we got to look at all the main American brands from Gap to Banana Republic, and some of the British names from FCUK to Ted Baker, which made us laugh when we saw them. Then, in a city where people dream of becoming millionaires at the turn of a card, there are all the other shops that can take that million right back if you do. Prada, Gucci,

Ralph Lauren, Armani – they're all there. So too are the jewellery stores – which is where the paparazzi found us and started yet another stupid rumour.

Charlotte likes jewellery. Comparing rings and bracelets and necklaces that all look alike to me after a while isn't my favourite occupation. But, like every other boyfriend or husband in the world I know, I have to go along with things sometimes and try and look enthusiastic at the right times and say the right things.

That's exactly what I was doing in Vegas until I decided I desperately needed a cigarette. The great thing about that place is that you don't really need to worry about where you can and can't smoke like you do in loads of other parts of America. People are walking round even the poshest shops carrying beers or plastic cups full of spirits, so a quick drag isn't going to bother anyone.

As if having a burst of nicotine wasn't bad enough, I also had a bit of a flirt with some shop girls to pass the time. Is it wrong to flirt like that? I don't know. Am I a flirt? Yes I am, always have been. I see it as a bit of harmless fun. It doesn't mean anything, but it makes me feel good, and hopefully it brightens up other people's days too. I'm a lot shyer than most people realise – I get tongue-tied, sometimes, talking to girls I fancy. But what I can do is smile. I love cheeky grins, a bit of eye contact, making it obvious you fancy someone, even though it's just as obvious you're not going to do anything about it.

So that's how it began in the shopping mall. A grin or two, a quick look, then another one. That kind of thing makes me feel alive. But I never forget I'm with my girlfriend and in a bizarre kind of way I think flirting is a bit of a compliment to her. If I saw good-looking guys checking Charlotte out, then it actually made me proud. It reminded me that other guys would love to get closer to my girlfriend but that they can't, because she's with me.

Persuading Charlotte that flirting is harmless and that it should make her feel stronger wasn't so easy. So we weren't the happiest couple in the world when we headed back to our hotel suite. I'd failed in every man's number-one duty as a boyfriend – to be interested in shopping and to pretend that no other woman exists. Things had been made even worse by the fact that the friendly shop assistants clearly hadn't got a clue who Charlotte was when she finally came out of the jewellery shop and joined me. The girl who so often wants to be a nobody, and who says she craves being anonymous and being treated just like any other 17-year-old, doesn't always like it when she gets her way.

Sometimes I did feel there was more than one Charlotte Church in the world: the private one I was alone with, laughed with and loved; and the public one who had to deal with fame and all the pressures and insecurities that came with it. It seemed as if the second Charlotte Church was with me that afternoon in Las Vegas.

Anyway, what we hadn't realised until too late was that the press had been all around us on our shopping trip as well. The paparazzi had got shots of me smoking outside the jewellery shop and they were a cue for yet another depressing little piece in the British tabloids.

'Charlotte Church was spotted dragging her "fiancé" Steven Johnson round jewellery shops in Las Vegas at the weekend,' said one of them. 'While she perused diamond rings costing around £15,000, he reportedly turned pale at the gills and wandered off for a cigarette. He shouldn't worry. I doubt very much he will be paying for it.'

So what was that all about? Writing the word 'fiancé' like that made it sound once again like I had some secret scheme to marry Charlotte and get my hands on her cash. But I wasn't Charlotte's fiancé, I never had been and at that point in Las Vegas it was still far too early in our relationship to even think about that kind of thing. We had a lot of pressures on us but we were hoping to make it for the long term. If we did want to get married, we had already said we would do it in our mid-20s – which still seemed like a lifetime away.

Still, I could have lived without reading yet another cleverly phrased way to make me look like a gold-digger. No, as the journalist said, I wouldn't be paying for a £15,000 diamond ring. But then neither would Charlotte. It's called window-shopping and everyone does it. All we were doing was having some fun, passing some time and dreaming some dreams, like everyone. What's so wrong with that?

Anyway, once we had sorted out our little tensions, Charlotte and I ordered some room service back in our suite and worked out what to do next. We spent well over an hour just standing in the street, holding hands and watching the fountains outside the Bellagio Hotel, which are designed to soar up and dance in time to music. But we weren't quite as relaxed as we should have been, because Charlotte was getting tense about the big Saturday-night show. She was also worried about her hair and what she was going to wear – unwittingly triggering another splash for the papers back home.

'You look good. I like it.'

'Well, I hate it. I can't wear it. I need a big new Las Vegas dress.'

Maybe it was because when you see how over-the-top Vegas is, you feel anything you have to wear is too pale and ordinary in comparison. But whatever the reason, Charlotte was almost crying the next morning when she stood in the middle of our room looking at the outfit she had planned to wear for the concert.

'Honestly, Charl, it looks great,' I offered, genuinely convinced she would look a million dollars when she wore it on the night.

'I can't go on stage in that. Not here. I need something else.' Charlotte scrunched the dress up and threw it on to the wardrobe floor. She had made up her mind, so we got ready to hit the shops again.

After trying on what seemed like a million different dresses, Charlotte found the one she wanted. It was by a designer called Roberto Cavalli and, while it looked fantastic, there was one small problem. It cost $7,000 and Charlotte wasn't allowed so spend anything like that much without permission from her managers. After a bit of argument they gave us their approval, because they could get the money out of Charlotte's trust fund by putting it down as a tour expense – personal spending like that was still totally off-limits for Charlotte.

'It's stunning, just what I need. I've got my confidence back now,' Charlotte said as we headed back to our rooms. So if you can put a price on peace of mind the new dress was worth every cent.

As usual, I was backstage with Charlotte when the Las Vegas show began. I had long since got used to the way she felt before a performance and I could read her moods without either of us saying a word. So I knew when she wanted me in the room, either to talk to or just to be there, and I knew instinctively when she wanted to be on her own or to have some privacy. It meant that I wandered around the back-of-house area quite a bit, nosing around, checking things out, seeing who was doing what. The sheer logistics of a big concert like this almost defy belief, especially in Las Vegas, where money doesn't seem to matter. It was like there was a whole secret city behind the scenes putting everything together. And I have to admit I felt cool that everyone knew I was going out with the star of the show and that my job was to make sure she was calm and relaxed enough to give her best. That was the role and the label I liked to have, and it was one that only people who knew me or saw the two of us together ever gave me.

But, while I liked the people I met well enough that night, I have to admit that at this 'one night only' concert I thought things had been misjudged from the start. The show was billed to open at 8pm, people had been taking their seats from about 7pm and there was a real sense of anticipation in the air. So did it really make sense to put a handful of guitar players and drummer on stage at the start of the show – and to keep them there playing away for nearly an hour? Big sections of the vast crowd certainly didn't think so, even though I think one of the guitarists was famous in his own right. In Britain there would have been slow handclaps, but in America fans just started chanting Charlotte's name to get the message across. They wanted the main event and I was worried that if they were forced to wait any longer they would be in an angry mood when she finally came on. I knew Charlotte would be worried, as well – she would have an even higher mountain to climb to charm them if they were in a bad mood.

Fortunately Charlotte can charm the birds out of the trees when she puts her mind to it. The applause was amazing when the lights dimmed and she finally stepped out of the wings, hair up in big curls, that brand new dress glimmering as a thousand camera flashes sparked off across the auditorium. She had decided to take things from the top – walking on singing 'Tonight' from the musical *West Side Story*.

After that came the charm. She told stories about how much she loved Las Vegas – especially the shopping – and admitted she'd only bought her dress there that afternoon. I'm not sure why that was so fascinating, but the audience went wild. I suppose she was being honest, refreshing and, well, a teenager. People liked her – even though backstage I could tell a lot of people had trouble with her accent and how fast she was speaking.

The rest of her set was a very adult, very mellow affair. Sting is one of Charlotte's heroes, and after a few more show tunes she did a fantastic version of his 'Fields of Gold'. Then, her worst professional nightmare. Missing cues and forgetting lines is Charlotte's big fear in rehearsals, but she normally gets those fears out of her system before the audience shows up and she gets it all right on the night. Except for this particular night.

The orchestra was doing the introduction to one new track and, while I didn't spot it myself because it's not my kind of music, it turned out that she had done what she was most worried about. Everyone got a bit embarrassed, the orchestra stopped, the conductor froze and Charlotte couldn't believe it.

'Did I just mess up? Did I just miss something? Oh, my God, I've just made a huge, huge mistake, everyone. I'm so sorry,' she said, thinking she had been humiliated in front of 7,000 people who had paid up to $100 for a ticket. But, of course, everyone forgave her immediately because she was so happy to admit she had screwed up. Even backstage we were laughing – with Charlotte, not at her. When the orchestra gave it another try and her voice came in at just the right time there were even some supportive little claps in the audience. She was flying now and she'd scored a hit in this toughest of entertainment towns.

I had heard the rest of her songs loads of times and while stuff like 'Amazing Grace' doesn't really set me alight, other songs like REM's 'Everybody Hurts' were just great. I remember kissing Charlotte as she came off stage at the end of the show, knowing she would be called back on for an encore. It's another of Charlotte's nightmares that audiences won't be that bothered about her performance and will get their things and leave the moment she goes off stage. In Las Vegas, however, I could see in her eyes that she felt a real rush when it was obvious that no one was leaving till she had sung some more.

'They love you. You've done it!' I said as my Charlotte turned and headed back into the spotlights. I think one of the songs she did as an encore was 'Danny Boy' which as a proud Welshman I thought was kind of cool in a place like Las Vegas.

In her dressing room after the final curtain and the audience had headed back to the gambling tables and the slot machines, Charlotte was bouncing off the walls. 'Was it OK? Did it go OK? Did people really like it? Did I really mess up on that song when I missed the cue?' she kept asking. Charlotte's confidence as a performer always amazes me. She is good, and deep down she knows that she is. But she also needs a lot of reassurance after the event. I suppose every perfectionist is the same.

So what do superstars do after a big, successful show? I'm sure many of the 7,000 audience at the Aladdin – and the British 'super-fans', who make sure they see every concert Charlotte does, wait at the stage door and report back to each other – might think she was heading out to some lavish party. Well, the truth is that Charlotte just got grabbed by loads of industry people and had to carry on working until we finally got to make a break. At that point we just headed back to our room to open the mini bar and turn on the telly. Being Charlotte Church isn't always as glamorous as people think.

But we had some tense moments the next day, our last in Las Vegas. The hotel was over the moon about the way the concert had gone, so Charlotte was on a major high from that. The show had confirmed her status on the entertainment A-list in America as well as in Britain, but before we left I had some work to do for myself.

My dream, at that point, had been to be a success in my own right. I was so fed up of being attacked in the press for supposedly sponging off Charlotte and I desperately wanted to prove that I had something to offer too. I had set up a couple of meetings with some New York modelling and casting agents who were in town, but on the way there Charlotte had a bit of a panic attack, so we had to turn the limo around. Because of this in-car crisis my meetings got delayed, which was pretty upsetting.

When I finally got to meet the New York agents, I thought my dream might really come true. Yet at the back of my head was the nagging doubt whether Charlotte really wanted these meetings to lead to anything. I put those thoughts to one side, but they were something I would have to face up to in the future.

For now Charlotte and I were in yet another limo, being whisked to the hidden VIP area in Las Vegas International Airport. We were finally on our way back to Wales, back to where it had all begun.

CHAPTER TWO

CHILD STARS

Charlotte Church has often been seen as the ultimate child star, but oddly enough I reckon I was actually in the papers long before she was. My dad says I was only about four when he took a phone call from the *Daily Star*, of all papers. Apparently some research had come out showing that Cardiff was at that point Britain's most peaceful, multicultural city. It was after the race riots back in the 1980s had hit several other big British cities but never even threatened Cardiff.

The *Star* reporter wanted to do a feature on the way different cultures lived side by side in Wales – as you can tell, the paper then was very different to the way it is today. He had been asked to try and track down the biggest, most racially diverse family in Cardiff and, not surprisingly, he had been pointed in our direction.

All my life I have been part of a big, loving and strong family. The doors to our houses have always seemed to be open. Aunts, uncles, cousins, grandparents – they all come in and out all day every day to chat, catch up, borrow stuff, get a break from their own families, whatever they need. In a way it made me feel I never had just one home. I had loads of other homes I could go to, where I would get the same feeling of family.

Anyway, back then I also knew that families come in all different shapes and shades. We seemed to come in every colour you could imagine. But no one ever got judged on anything except the way they behaved and the kind of person they were. And that should be what life is all about.

Even looking back at the photograph now it is hard to count exactly how many of us got together in the local church hall for the photo shoot – we're all lined up and looking over each other's shoulders trying to make sure the camera can see us. All I very vaguely remember now is how much fun it was, and how it felt like a holiday or just another big gathering for the biggest, closest family in town.

Doing that story got us a label, as well – and for once it was a good one. 'The Rainbow Family' was what the *Star* called us, and we were held up as a great example of decent, hard-working, ordinary people. If only the press could have stuck to the facts like this rather than inventing quite different labels a dozen years later...

What that story also did was give a little picture of the type of environment I grew up in – an incredibly happy one. 'It began with a couple falling in love and a wedding that shocked the neighbourhood. Now, 67 years later, 100 multicoloured folk show Britain how to live in perfect harmony,' the paper began. 'The bride was aged just 16 and the groom was 40. But that wasn't all. The year was 1919 and nobody gave the marriage between Emily Ashford and Joseph Dixon a hope in hell. But today, 67 years later, the children, grandchildren and great-grandchildren of Joe and Emily live in cheerful family harmony in the docks area of Cardiff. Some are black. Some are white. Some are coffee. Some blond. Some ginger. And there are a whole lot who don't give a damn what they are.' Nearly 90 years since Joe and Emily met, and 20 years since the family picture was taken, the story is pretty much the same.

That first little brush with fame might seem small compared to what Charlotte was to experience in a few years' time. But amazingly enough the Johnson family was about to go global.

We didn't know a thing about it until it had happened, but around a year after the *Daily Star* piece was published and forgotten about, it was picked up by the *National Enquirer* in America. For some reason their reporters had been doing some digging into our family tree and had tracked down more information about Joseph Dixon, the black coal miner from Virginia who had sailed over to Bristol to find work in Britain in 1903. They also told American readers more about the white woman he had met, fallen in love with and started this ever-growing rainbow family with.

That *National Enquirer* story turned us into an even bigger family group. The Virginia branch got in touch with the Welsh crowd and formed a new alliance across the Atlantic that continues to this day.

Other people in my family have also done great things. For example, my uncle Colin Dixon got 13 caps playing rugby league for Great Britain and set a world record transfer fee in the 1960s. A cousin, Steve Robinson, was WBO World Featherweight boxing champion in 1995 and defended his world title seven times in the 1990s. Almost a dozen other cousins have also played rugby for Cardiff and Wales over the years and some of my nephews look likely to follow in their footsteps. We've also done well on the music and literary front – another relative, Laverne Brown, was a great R&B singer, and an aunt researched even deeper into our family history and had a book published on the subject: *Yesterday, Today and Tomorrow*.

While I was living with my mum, dad and sisters near the docks, Charlotte was experiencing a completely different type of family life in the equally working-class Fairwater district of Cardiff. Her real dad – of whom more later – had left before Charlotte was two and her mum had since met James Church, the man who would formally adopt her daughter and give her the Church name. He already had two children, but as they lived with their mother, Charlotte was effectively brought up as an only child. She told me it was a lot quieter in her house than it ever was in mine.

Over at the Johnsons we made a lot of noise because there were so many of us. As blokes, Dad and I were totally outnumbered. I had a twin sister, Samira, and three other sisters, Michaela, Soraya and Shakira, all of whom I still see almost every day. Back then Mum and Dad both worked – Dad in particular had got lucky by setting up a mobile phone repair business just at the point when mobiles were starting to take off.

At the start I think the idea had been for all of us kids to go to private schools, because Mum and Dad really wanted us to make the most of our lives. But as the family grew, the bills got too high and Samira and I ended up going to our local schools just across the park instead.

You might never believe it from all the newspaper articles calling me a 'teenage tearaway' and worse, but I actually had a really good time at school. I played football, rugby, tried to get into the school swimming team and made some great friends that I still have today. On the grades front I was also doing pretty well. I wasn't top of the class but I got pretty close and I was hoping to do well in all my exams. In fact, I actually got moved up the ladder and took two exams a year early in Form 4.

Apart from Music, the other subjects I was good at and most interested in were Design Technology and Maths. I was also pretty keen on computing. I had this dream that if I really worked hard at it, I could be one of those hackers who set warning bells ringing in government departments, at NASA or in big banks.

But then my mum and dad decided to split up, and it affected me deeply. Something about my dad moving out of our house and leaving me the only man there made me feel rebellious. I felt like I had to be in charge of everyone, like I had to grow up really fast, when really I wanted the opposite. I wanted everything to be the way it always had been, and if it couldn't be, then I wanted to lash out.

I had a sort of amateur music studio in a shed in the garden and I started spending more and more time there. I worked longer, louder and later on my music – until the neighbours started to complain about the noise. Some of my mates had motorbikes, though we weren't all old enough to ride them. But it seemed cool to forget about school and just head off on the bikes for a day of freedom. It was about the time when other people were quitting school altogether and suddenly that seemed tempting to me as well. I met my dad in the street one day and he told me I had to get my act together and grow up. But I couldn't or wouldn't hear it, and I carried on acting like a kid and falling behind.

What makes it seem all the more stupid now is that the split between my mum and dad was incredibly amicable. There were no scenes, no shouting and no real stress, and they've pretty much managed to stay on good terms. Dad got a house a few streets away, which he would spend the next couple of years gutting and rebuilding before I moved in with him. I don't know what happens in private; they certainly never fight in public and they are both 100 per cent part of all their children's lives. It was surely the most civilised and grown-up separation you could imagine and there was never any question of us kids having to take sides or face some of the really tough stuff that other kids of divorcing parents have to do.

But I did get off track when it happened. I pretty much lost interest at school, stopped studying, stopped paying attention and after a while stopped turning up. Then, when things started to go downhill at school, I felt I just had to get out. So I left and, having been ahead of the game, I started to fall behind. My mum and dad were furious, but they had problems of their own and neither they nor my sisters could persuade me I was making a mistake.

For quite a while I thought I was going to prove them wrong anyway. I'd been DJ'ing at friends' parties for years and suddenly found I could make money doing it in pubs, clubs and private parties. Throw in some earnings from my dad's phone business and things didn't seem to be going so badly. Who needed proper qualifications? I was a teenager without a real care in the world so it was easy to think that they don't matter. All my life seemed to be about back then was having fun with my mates, doing up cars, meeting girls and showing off.

One year a big group of friends had decided to head out to Ibiza on a trip and I decided to join them. Some of them only stayed for a week or two. I loved the island from the moment I saw the sun, the sea, the beach bars and the women. I asked around, got some bar work and told everyone I met about my DJ'ing back in Cardiff. That paid off in the end and I got some gigs out there. I stayed two months in the end, working in bars and on boats, and came back happy, chilled and ready for a fresh start.

Going away on your own has to be a good thing for most teenagers. Staying away beyond the length of a standard holiday certainly is. It teaches you to fend for yourself and shows you that you can make it. I wasn't doing any serious jobs out in Ibiza, but I still grew up while I was working in the bars there to pay my rent. It taught me that life can't just be about sunshine and checking out the next planeload of babes in bikinis. I had fun, but I finally realised I had to get serious about the future, and that meant catching up with all the people who hadn't left school at 15 like me. I was back on track.

Back at home I got accepted on to a computer-programming course at college. It was a two-year course, hopefully ending in an HND qualification. I dreamed of working for someone like Microsoft at the end of it. Lots of my fellow students were good people and I started to enjoy my new, more settled life. I was still DJ'ing and working part time for my dad's mobile phone business, so I had plenty of cash in my pockets.

I also found out about a government-sponsored training scheme in the music industry. It was backed by the Intech organisation and competition was fierce for places, so I pulled out all the stops with my application to be part of it. The selectors must have seen some potential in me and once on board I found myself being paid a decent weekly amount to produce tracks in its studios and learn about every element of the music business. It was a dream come true for someone like me. These were fantastic times, and after my wobble leaving school early I suddenly had a hell of a lot of opportunities opening up for me. A year or so later Intech was going to offer me even more work options. Charlotte was never going to be the only one of us with a busy career.

Which brings me to Charlotte herself and the night we met.

CHAPTER THREE

ONE NIGHT IN CARDIFF

At the start of 2002, Charlotte was big news, but for a rather sleazy reason. Someone, somewhere had set up a website counting down the days and hours until her 16th birthday, because this was when she could legally have sex. There always seemed to have been a 'dirty old man' interest in Charlotte, in her body and in what she could do with it.

At this stage Charlotte Church and her music weren't exactly a big part of my home life. My dad is the biggest music fan around, but he listens to Bob Marley, reggae, jazz, blues and stuff like that. Classical music didn't figure much in our part of town. The only voice of an angel we would hear would be a Hell's Angel, as the old joke goes.

Like everyone else in Cardiff I knew who Charlotte was, but that was as far as it went. If I ever had any thoughts on what kind of person she might be, I would probably have put her down as stuck-up, full of herself, arrogant, a spoiled little rich kid. I forgot that she was actually from a tough working-class background just like mine – I would only ever picture her in a big new house with a flash lifestyle. I couldn't have seen someone like that getting on with my family or my mates, and I couldn't imagine going out with someone who didn't do that. Anyway, I had just split up with my girlfriend and wasn't really looking for a new one.

Is it arrogant to say that I've always had an eye for women and never had a lot of trouble getting them to like me? I can't say I have any idea why I sometimes get lucky when other blokes fail. I don't look at myself in the mirror and think I look especially good or different. I try hard with my appearance and like every other guy my age I'm into having the best kit and the right look. But apart from that I see myself as just like any other lad with a roving eye and a bit of attitude. Maybe girls like that.

What I do know is that there were loads of gorgeous women at one party where I was helping with the DJ'ing in February 2002. I was in full Jack the Lad mode that night, making eye contact with as many women as possible, even though I was working and couldn't do much more than that. One of those girls was Charlotte Church.

I felt like the coolest guy in the room and that was how a lot of people treated me. If things are going well at a party the DJ is always going to be the king, as anyone from Norman Cook to Mylo will tell you. The

DJ is the guy the girls want to get close to because he's running the show. I loved the rush you get from that. I like the fact that you're getting respect for doing something well, being at the top of your game.

That has to be a feeling Charlotte recognises herself. On the work front she likes controlling a room as well, so we had another link right from the start. What we didn't have was any opportunity to talk. Charlotte was just a face in a big, busy crowd. I was just the guy playing the music at the back of the room. It could have ended right there.

Our first real connection came through some of my college and her school friends at that party. Someone told me the other day that Cardiff is now the fastest-growing city in Europe, but back then it seemed a pretty small place and everyone's worlds overlapped when you took family, friends and other connections into account. A few weeks later my world overlapped with Charlotte's again when she and a group of friends from that party went to the cinema a few streets away from my dad's house.

'Steve, we're round the corner. Can we come over?'

One of my mates had been to see the same film and the whole gang had got together outside the cinema at about half past ten looking for somewhere to go for a while. He knew that my open-plan attic room at the top of our house would be an ideal place and, without knowing exactly who these girls were, I put out the invitation. Dad and a friend of his were downstairs sitting round the dining-room table chewing the fat when the door-bell rang and everyone trooped in. The group, five girls and three of my mates, all headed up the two flights of stairs to my room, where the music was playing.

I seem to remember thinking they were all looking pretty smart for a night at the cinema, but Charlotte marched into the room and just threw herself down on my bed, looking out through the skylights into the night. She was anything but spoiled or stuck up. After a while, I got talking to her and that was when it all started to go right.

Forget classical crap and opera. Right away I realised that this wasn't what really made Charlotte tick. I found out that what she did care about was R&B music. She knew my kind of music. She had opinions on it. She had favourites. She knew as much music trivia and detail as I did. And that, I have to say, attracted me more than anything. Looking around my room – heating up now with so many people in it, cigarette smoke rising and music playing – I suddenly felt pretty damn good.

Yes, it was cool to have someone famous in my bedroom – everyone's a bit star-struck and I defy anyone not to get some kind of thrill out of meeting people like that. But what was cooler to me that night was the fact that I'd actually connected with Charlotte about something as important as music. I love it when I meet someone who shares my interests and I wanted to carry on talking all night. I was thinking of tracks she might like, of bands she might want to go and see. I was making plans – but then a mobile phone started to ring. It was Charlotte's and for some reason everybody had to go.

'Charlotte's really cool. Is she seeing anybody? Can I get her number?' I asked one of the other girls, Becky, in a panic at the top of the stairs as everyone milled around getting their coats and bags. I didn't get the number because there were too many people around and it wouldn't have looked cool. But I kissed Charlotte goodbye.

Now, I could say that our first kiss was passionate and perfect, and pretend that we were Romeo and Juliet. But in reality it was all a bit of a mess. I was pissed off that she was leaving when I felt we had so much more to say, and I was worried that we might never get another chance to say it. But I didn't want to look too keen in front of either my mates or hers if I'd read things wrong and she wasn't really interested. So our goodbye kiss was somewhere between embarrassing and humiliating. Still, I guess that most teenagers would say the same about their first big love affair.

Anyway, the end result was that the girls had all gone and I wasn't feeling too great about it. Dad was pretty impressed when I told him Charlotte had been one of the girls in the group, but it's a credit to how down-to-earth she is that he wasn't sure which one of them she'd been. But he was going to get a second chance to find out, because at about 2am my mobile went and it was them.

It turned out they'd only been down one of the local bars and now they wanted to start the party all over again. This time it was just Charlotte, Becky and a couple of others, so we turned the music down and just spent the next hour chilling before they decided that this time they really did have to leave. At that point I decided I had to make a better attempt to get Charlotte's attention, and that I might as well be direct.

'So, have you got a boyfriend?' I whispered on the landing.

'No,' she said, suddenly shy.

'Can I have a proper kiss?'

And she said that I could.

What I remember now is how much Charlotte started to shake when I put my arms around her and pulled her face close to mine. She was nervous, excited, but very happy to be there. And no way was it a one-sided kiss. I couldn't have felt better. If you take away our shared interest in music, then the things I liked about Charlotte most were her eyes, her face and her figure. Her eyes were big, wide and green. They were somehow confident and shy at the same time. I wanted to spend more time looking into them. Her face was just so fresh, so open, so alive. And her figure? Neither of us knew it then, but within six months Charlotte was going to be named 'Rear of the Year'. I probably don't need to add much more to that, but I will say she looked just as good and turned me on just as much from the front.

But would I ever see her again? I still hadn't got her number and as the next week began I was back at college as normal. Two days passed and nothing. Then I got a call from a college friend, Dilly, who had another friend who was planning a party when her mum was away. Charlotte was going to be there and apparently she had asked if the DJ from the docks could be invited as well. The whole thing felt like the most childish, teenage set-up you could imagine – and I didn't mind it one little bit.

It was an afternoon party with a decent mix of old mates and complete strangers who must have been friends of friends. But the rest of the guest list hardly mattered: it was about me and Charlotte and all we really wanted to do was kiss.

I could tell Charlotte was still nervous about things, though she didn't shake as much as she had done in the early hours of Sunday morning. She also didn't let me have as much fun with my hands as I would have liked, but I was more than happy to take things at her pace. It just felt so good to be with a sexy girl that I knew I could talk to about music whenever the kissing stopped.

At that point I don't think Charlotte or I needed any encouragement to see each other again, but we were going to get some help anyway. There really had been love in the air that night at my dad's house while Charlotte and I had been sitting in the corner talking about music. My mate Joshua had hit it off with Naomi, one of Charlotte's best friends. A strong little foursome was being born, and not surprisingly the next time I saw Charlotte was at Naomi's house a couple of days later.

So how did I woo Charlotte, the teenage millionaire? Did I take her to expensive restaurants, buy her jewellery or drive her around in a flash sports car? Not quite. We spent that day hanging around on street corners, sitting on walls, watching people go by, kissing, talking, both being 100 per cent ordinary. It was nice, relaxed and secure. We were all perfectly safe, fantastically happy. If only things could have stayed that way.

CHAPTER FOUR

THE BIRTHDAY PARTY

Not everyone's girlfriend has to cancel dates in the first few weeks of their relationship because she's got meetings with film producers about her first Hollywood movie. But that's how things began with Charlotte and I can't say I blamed her for being excited.

Apparently she had been talking for ages about making a break into films, but had been waiting for the right project to come along. And for someone who had spent so much of her childhood on the road and who was getting ready to sit her GCSEs, the right first project had to be local.

The opportunity came up with *I'll Be There*, which was to be made by Warner Brothers, so it was a really big deal. As we sat on walls and park benches on cold early April days, Charlotte told me about the script, which couldn't have been more perfect for her. The idea was that she would play a teenage singer who tracks down the dad who doesn't even know she exists and tries to get him back together with her mother.

The full casting hadn't been agreed upon, but Charlotte mentioned the likes of Jemma Redgrave and Joss Ackland for some of the other roles. I probably I tried to pretend I knew who she was talking about, but I didn't need to pretend I shared her excitement. She was thrilled this gig could come off, worried that she might not be up for the acting part, and desperately looking forward to trying something new. It was brilliant to see her so happy and we joked about learning her lines together at my house and practising her moves out in the park. I even got Charlotte to deliver a joke acceptance speech for the Oscars. You know, just in case...

The film was going to take a while to get the green light, so Charlotte was going to be at a lot of meetings while they tried to sort everything out. Thank God for texting and mobile telephones. If we couldn't actually see each other, then we made sure that we communicated every day, loads of times a day. It turned out that we had more and more in common, and we were desperate to spend whatever time we could together.

One night, just before ten, I got a call saying Charlotte was around the corner at the five-star St David's Hotel. She was in yet more meetings about the film but had a break and wanted to know if I could get over there fast. I was on my way before she had even hung up the phone. I rang up as I came round the final corner and Charlotte actually ran out of the hotel doors to meet me. God, she looked so beautiful that night, wearing a top, stylish dress, her long hair perfect and professionally styled. It was a glossy, totally different Charlotte to the one who had flopped down on my bed with her mates a few weeks earlier. But it was one I would easily fall for just the same.

But even then I got a reminder that seeing Charlotte wasn't like seeing any of my previous girlfriends. Two bodyguards were loitering around the hotel doors, watching me carefully and looking very out of place. Little did I know that this was something I would have to get used to.

We kissed, of course, though both of us were pretty embarrassed about being watched. Charlotte told me how her meetings were going, about how boring some of the people were and how much she wanted to leave. But she couldn't, and after less than ten minutes she had to head back into the hotel.

Before she went, however, she told me something. She was planning a big 16th birthday party in town and would I be there? Suddenly our little play-dating, texting, phoning and hanging out seemed a bit more serious. This was a big night for her. It would be our first proper, official date, so it would be a big night for me too.

I agreed, of course, because I wanted to be anywhere that Charlotte was. But I had another reason for wanting to be at the party. Despite how close we had become, I had heard a few rumours from mates and people at college that Charlotte was actually seeing someone else. Going to her 16th birthday party would put this worry to bed one way or the other. If the rumour was true the guy would either be there and it would be obvious, or he wouldn't and I'd be the man. I wouldn't have missed the event for the world. But when the big day came, I very nearly did.

The party was at a bar and nightclub place called Continentals in the town centre and it began pretty early. But my mates and I don't normally get to places till 10pm or so and I didn't want to change things and look too keen for Charlotte. Maybe I was an idiot, but looking cool still mattered to me. Charlotte was not impressed and I probably pissed her off and took the shine off her night. She rang and texted me to find out where I was and in the end my mates and I got the message and headed over there some time after 10pm. It turned out we knew some of the guys doing security on the door so we had a bit of a chat before finally heading inside.

There were about 200 people at the party, but one of the very first things I saw when we got there was Charlotte herself. She was dancing. And she looked bloody good. She had a short skirt on and, while she doesn't like them, her legs looked fantastic.

I didn't join her on the dance floor, though, because I was the cool DJ, remember? My mates and I hung around, all watching her, and I loved it when I thought she was putting on a bit of a show just for me and trying to move the action closer to wherever I was standing. But in the end I couldn't resist her and we ended up in a corner of the bar, kissing, feeling great just to be so close together.

In my mind, Charlotte, your birthday party was when our relationship officially began. It was when we first got serious and got committed to each other. The other guy that I had been told about didn't seem to exist. I was convinced we could have a great time together. You were fun and you were sexy. What could possibly go wrong?

Fortunately I wasn't going to find out straight away, because the day after the party Charlotte was back to work and off on her travels. Her first stop was Los Angeles, where she had some meetings and celebrated her actual birthday with some girlfriends in a celebrity restaurant. Then she was off to Salt Lake City to sing for the closing ceremony of the Winter Olympics – amazing stuff for a 16-year-old from south Wales.

We kept on speaking and texting every day, though – sometimes talking about everything and nothing for as long as an hour at a time. Back at college I was over the moon about this new relationship, though I was determined to keep it under wraps in case it all went wrong. I couldn't wait for Charlotte to get back from her trip and I just kept on planning places we could go and things we could do. I even went as far as sorting out hours of music that I thought she would like and that I wanted to play for her when she was back. Then, one morning my mobile went off during a break in classes. I was getting my first wake-up call about what it was like to date a celebrity.

'Hello, is that Steve Johnson? I'm a reporter from the *News of the World* and if you've got a few minutes I want to talk to you a little bit about Charlotte Church.'

'Yeah right, mate. Who is this?'

'Like I said, I'm a reporter from the *News of the World*. Do you have a few minutes now to talk to us about Charlotte?'

'Get off, mate. Who is this? You're winding me up.'

Looking back, was this when my relationship with the press got set in stone? Would this one conversation colour how I was to be written about ever after? It seemed unbelievable to me that a reporter from a paper like the *News of the World* in London could be ringing a guy like me up on his mobile. I didn't know how people like that could get my number: I was just a Welsh teenager on a computer course with a new girlfriend. I knew absolutely nothing about the media and the way it worked. I thought the phone call was from a mate taking the piss, so I didn't exactly watch my language when he kept on asking me questions. I said stupid things because I thought I was having a laugh with a mate round the corner. I had no idea that everything I said was being recorded and written down hundreds of miles away in London.

The article the *News of the Screws* wrote about me duly

reflected all that bravado and naivety. So did the picture of me that they printed alongside it.

CHARLOTTE CHURCH DATES TEENAGE TEARAWAY, was the headline. It ran over a picture of Charlotte looking as sweet and angelic as ever. Then one of me, where for some bizarre reason they had half-shaded out my face, so I looked like one of the criminals you see being taken to court where they've done something so awful we're not allowed to see what they look like. If I didn't know the real me, I'd have said the guy in the picture was a thug, a criminal, a lout – not a computer student who'd never come close to being in trouble with the law in his life.

'Charlotte, I can't believe it. Some reporter has written an article about us. And it's terrible.'

I called her that weekend with the paper open in front of me. At that point all I was worried about was her. I didn't want to have somehow pissed her off by having accidentally spoken to the press. I didn't want my stupidity to have killed our relationship before it even got off the ground. At that point I had no idea that I would end up as the victim of this sort of article. I didn't see that the headline and the blacked-out picture would be the first every other newspaper reporter would know of me and that it would give them the opening lines to all the stories that were to come.

'Don't worry, Steve,' Charlotte said. 'The press has been desperate to put me with a boyfriend for years now. It'll blow over. We can sort it when I get back home.' And after a while, when I had read out more of the article to her, she began to show me what felt like the funny side of it all. We started to laugh about it. We felt like we were two outlaws up against the world. This wasn't going to beat us, we said. It wasn't even going to affect us. We promised that we would fight off the press together and we'd win.

A couple of days after that first bizarre article was printed, Charlotte was back in Cardiff, looking tanned, healthy and as sexy as ever. It turned out that her mum and dad were out for the night and she was up for a bit of a party at home. Charlotte's success had meant the Church family had long since been able to move out of their two-up two-down terraced home in Fairwater. Now they were living in a flash, five-bedroom, multi-bathroom detached house in the posh Coryton part of town. The house had proper security, of course, including big walls and big high gates to the drive and parking for loads of cars. It wasn't Hollywood or *Footballers' Wives*-style huge, but it wasn't bad for a 16-year-old and it intimidated the hell out of us all.

Charlotte and her friends had obviously been having a good girlie night in by the time my mates and I got there at about 10pm, and there was plenty of smoke and empty bottles lying around to prove it. We kissed hello, of course, and tried to be as close to each other as possible as someone turned up the music. Charlotte's friend Naomi and my mate Joshua were both there and I pretty much knew everyone in the room. But what I really wanted was to get Charlotte into a different room – ideally one with a bed in it.

'Steve. Follow me.'

Three little words, and my wish came true.

Charlotte had a room right at the top of the house just like I did, though you could hardly call hers an attic room. For a start, there was a four-poster bed in it. And to be honest, that was exactly where I wanted us to end up.

That night was so slow and so perfect. While I could tell Charlotte knew just what she wanted to do, I could also tell that she wanted me to be the one to control it and push it forward. Sometimes, for a while, she started shaking again, like she had done that time we had kissed properly back at my house. But kissing her face and her neck very softly and running my hands round her back and round her body seemed to calm her down again.

Charlotte's eyes drove me wild. They were so wide, so beautiful, so scared and yet so ready. We rolled around on the bed, touching, feeling, sometimes laughing, taking it slow, making it last. I couldn't have been more ready myself that night. I wanted to take off Charlotte's clothes, slowly, with my hands and my teeth. I wanted to see her body. I wanted, more than anything, to be naked with her and to have her sleep in my arms.

Unfortunately we both knew that there were two little problems. The first was that all our mates were downstairs. The second was that her mum and dad were due back soon and that this would not be a good way for me to meet the family. So, for that night at least, our clothes stayed on and our secrets were safe. But I knew Charlotte was thinking exactly the same as I was. We were right for each other and we were ready to go further. It was only a matter of finding the time and choosing the place to do it.

CHAPTER FIVE

WHERE'S YOUR MOTHER, CHARLOTTE?

By the time I met Charlotte, I'd had my share of flings and had got pretty serious with some girls. But I was hardly qualified to know exactly what step you take and when.

What I did know, however, was that when you got serious with a girl you tended to meet her family. It could be an ordeal, it might be stressful on both sides, but your girlfriend's mum, at least, normally wanted to know who her daughter was seeing every night. So why did Charlotte's parents never want to meet me?

My family were certainly keen enough to meet Charlotte – and not just because she was famous. My sister Michaela had helped me get through things when my last serious girlfriend had ended. She had seen how upset I had been and she wanted to make sure I wasn't risking the same sort of rejection again, so she wanted a first-hand view of what kind of girl Charlotte was. Charlotte soon got the seal of approval and the two of them were quite happy chatting away with each other in the house when I was on the phone or cooking or upstairs.

My mum and dad were equally keen to meet Charlotte, just like they had wanted to meet any other girls I had dated. As I still spent a lot of time at my mum's house, just around a few corners from my dad's, Charlotte got the once-over there very early on in our relationship. Thankfully my mum seemed to like her and the pair of them always got on pretty well. My old makeshift recording studio was still in my mum's shed and over the next few months Charlotte and I would spend a lot of time there fooling around with different tracks and sounds, heading back to my mum's kitchen whenever we got hungry. We spent quite a few nights at my mum's as well. It gave us a secret little base that the press never really found out about, and we knew we could always go there if the heat got too much at my dad's.

Weirdly enough, even Charlotte's friend Naomi's mother wanted to meet me and see what I was like – because I was the best mate of her daughter's new boyfriend. Happily I seemed to pass her tests and we're still happy to talk if we bump into each other in Cardiff to this day. Charlotte's mum kept her distance, however.

Back in my house Charlotte's toughest job was impressing my dad. He was no big fan of the Church family, and of Charlotte's mother in particular. In

Cardiff's small world he knew loads of people who had told him what Maria was like and how she acted – both before and after her daughter became a star. What he had heard and seen with his own eyes didn't impress him.

Charlotte and I were simply happy getting to know each other at this point. But at the back of both our minds I think we realised that both of our families could be a problem. We just didn't know how much of a problem.

Of course all my dad saw of Charlotte in those first days was a face at the door and the back of a head as she went upstairs to my room, often just a blur in the crowd. But when we became serious, she got a proper introduction and got to hang out downstairs when it was just me, her and my dad in the house. His verdict? 'I like her the way she is now,' he said one day when we were alone, 'but if she turns into her mother then your life will be hell.'

Fortunately, for the next year Charlotte was going to do everything she could to distance herself from the mother who had helped get her in front of the cameras and who had taken her on the road at 11. Unfortunately I was gradually to see that my dad's prophecy about human nature was going to come horribly true. The Charlotte Church I see and read about now looks and sounds very like the Maria Church my dad warned me about.

But back in 2002, as a cocky 17-year-old who was

falling in love, there were two main reasons why I dismissed my dad's fears. For a start, the Charlotte I knew then seemed pretty much perfect. Secondly, I'd never met her mother, so I had no idea how things would turn out if genetics did their stuff.

Looking back, I suppose the main reason why Charlotte's parents didn't want to meet and get to know me was that they thought they knew me already. They'd read the papers, and that had given them enough so-called information to feed their prejudices. According to the reporters I was bad, black, poor and trouble – four things the respectable householders of Coryton almost certainly didn't want in their neighbourhood.

But there was something else. William Hall, who wrote a book on Charlotte's early life, had a theory as well. 'Maria refuses to meet Johnson because he brings back dark memories of her own childhood sweetheart, another Stephen – Stephen Reed,' the *Daily Mirror's* Barbara Davies wrote after speaking to the writer. 'He was the man who made her pregnant when she was not much older than Charlotte and then abandoned her. Now she could be forgiven for fearing that history may repeat itself. I should imagine that every time Maria thinks about Stephen Johnson she is haunted by her own memories of Stephen Reed,' the article went on. 'Maria would view Charlotte's father as a tremendous mistake, although she had a beautiful daughter. She doesn't want Charlotte to make that kind of mistake herself.'

One result of it all was that Charlotte started spending more and more time over at mine and she started telling me just how unhappy she was at home.

Charlotte had been famous and had been making money for five years by the time I met her. Back in 1986, when she was born Charlotte Maria Church in a tiny terraced house in Llandaff, Cardiff, her roots were very much like mine, though the Church family don't like to focus on that. Her dad left soon afterwards and Charlotte told me that she's had next to nothing to do with him ever since. Her mum worked for the local council and ultimately married James, the man Charlotte calls her dad.

Even as a small child, I'm told, Charlotte had an amazing singing voice and the family struggled to pay for music lessons to develop it. She was in the choir at the local Cathedral School and got a scholarship for the private Howells school, which had a real reputation for music. Apparently Charlotte felt out of place there from the start, embarrassed when her parents drove her there in their battered old car and parked it alongside all the flash motors of the far richer families in her class.

Charlotte made her first bid for fortune, fame and freedom when she sang down the phone to the *Talking Telephone Numbers* show in 1997, which got her on the *Richard and Judy* show. She got a bigger break a few months later when she went on *The Big Big Talent Show* to introduce a performance by her aunt, Caroline

Cooper. Not really knowing what to expect, show host Jonathan Ross asked the 11-year-old sitting in front of him to sing a few lines before her aunt took the stage. Charlotte stood up, took a deep breath and sang *Pie Jesu* – part of the Andrew Lloyd-Webber song that would be her signature for years. A star was born.

'Look at my hair! What the hell am I wearing? I look like a baby.'

'Jonathan Ross looks like he's going to fall over.'

'I look like my head is going to explode.'

Charlotte and I sat and watched some of her old videos on television one night – and boy has she changed since then. At the time Jonathan Ross, like his audience, was gobsmacked and Charlotte's poor aunt was pretty much forgotten.

Next on the scene came super-agent Jonathan Shalit, who was told about Charlotte by *Popstars* judge Nigel Lythgoe. Shalit is a man I ended up having a lot in common with, as his rows with Charlotte's mum grew more and more intense. Jonathan, a decent bloke who I still respect, reckoned that Charlotte had the X-factor. He tracked down her parents and headed over to Wales to meet the family and hear Charlotte sing alongside her music teacher Louise Ryan.

'I closed my eyes and it was totally unreal,' he said later. 'I had this child in front of me, aged 11, with this amazing voice. It was a huge stunning voice. I knew at that moment, sitting on a sofa in Louise Ryan's study, that there was a superstar standing in front of me.'

Shalit set out to make that dream come true – though it didn't happen overnight. A load of record companies turned Charlotte down. But nearly a year later Sony spotted her potential and a five-album deal with a £100,000 advance was signed. Charlotte was in the studio and on the road from then on.

This was when Charlotte got the label that would cause so many problems by the time we got together. It was the title of her first album and meant she would forever be known as 'the voice of an angel'. By this point, only just a teenager, she was making some serious money and meeting some seriously important people, from the Queen and Prince Charles to the Pope and the President of the United States. She sang everywhere and for everyone. She got interviewed by the dullest people in Britain – Terry Wogan and all that crowd – and by the coolest ones in America – David Letterman was one early fan.

What Charlotte had also done was crack the American market, something few other current British acts have achieved. In 1999, for example, she had not one but two platinum albums in the States. It was incredible stuff and it built up both her name and her fortune. But none of this had come easy.

Charlotte told me she felt she was out of school as much as she was in it during those years, though she had tutors who travelled on the road with her and plenty of catch-up work to do every time she came back to Cardiff. What she also had all this time was her mum Maria on her back and waiting in the wings for every performance.

The more Charlotte talked to me about her life and her family, the more unhappy I realised she was. She would smile and laugh in public and tell the talk-show hosts that everything was fantastic. But I soon realised that inside she felt trapped on a treadmill, and that though it was understandable, it wasn't good to have your mother just two paces away almost 24 hours a day. In our early times together, loafing on the settee and eating takeaways at my dad's, watching DVDs and listening to music, Charlotte's unhappiness was just a shadow in the background. It was going to get a lot deeper. I hope I never again see a girl cry the way I saw Charlotte cry some nights after yet another long, awful phone conversation with her mother. But as the clocks went forward in the spring of 2002, all that was still to come. We still had adventures to have, and dreams to explore.

Being with Charlotte was always great fun. Pretty soon after we met she had been invited to do a fun run to raise money for the Noah's Ark children's hospital in Wales. Catherine Zeta Jones and Ian Botham were part of the fund-raising weekend and it was great to just get out, meet new people and feel I was slowly becoming part of her crazy celebrity world. Back at home I was getting used to Charlotte's late-night ways.

'It's me. Can I come over?'

I couldn't believe it the first time I got the call. It was

nearly midnight and I'd kissed Charlotte goodbye almost two hours earlier, after a group of us had been to the cinema. Now she said she was getting a cab and heading back across town to mine.

'You're crazy. What did you tell your mum?'

'Nothing. I climbed out of the window. They don't know I'm here.'

I stood in our living room looking at Charlotte in amazement. I thought I knew her pretty well at this point, but it turned out she could still surprise me.

'You're brave. Or crazy.'

'I don't care. This is where I want to be.'

And so she stayed for most of the night – many, many nights. Often we just cuddled, listened to music, talked away the hours under my skylight windows. Sometimes we really did fall asleep, fully clothed, on top of my bed. They were brilliant, secret times. And they always ended the same. Very early, normally before light, Charlotte would order a taxi and sneak back to her big house so her parents would be none the wiser. I knew then how much I loved Charlotte's spirit – and her determination.

At that point Charlotte was also being given the official confirmation that she was gorgeous: they were going to name her as 'Rear of the Year' alongside a *Coronation Street* actor who seems to have since disappeared. Looking back now, the whole idea of making a 16-year-old 'Rear of the Year' seems at least as sleazy as that 'countdown till Charlotte can have sex' website that her mother and her management were so keen to have closed down earlier. But in 2002, mother and management decided that Charlotte should head up to London, pull on some tight jeans and accept her award.

'Does my bum look big in those?'

'It doesn't matter. They picked you because you've got the best bum in Britain.'

God, we laughed at the newspaper articles and all the jokey headlines over the next few days. Charlotte's picture seemed to be everywhere and she said she had hardly ever seen as many photographers as she had on the day of the awards photocall.

'Charlotte has a great rear and is already taking steps to keep it that way,' we read that one of the guys who had judged the awards had said afterwards. We looked at each other in amazement. 'What is he talking about? Who is he and how could he possibly know anything about stuff like that?' Charlotte asked me, as we laughed at how ridiculous it had all become. It just felt like harmless fun and back in Cardiff it gave us one more reason to laugh at the rest of the world.

Right back from the beginning Charlotte's dirty laugh was one of the things I was most attracted to. I got her sense of humour that first night we spoke properly and she never stopped making me laugh afterwards. Even more brilliantly, she was able to make everyone else laugh as well. She was a guest on three main television shows in the first few months of our relationship: *Friday Night with Jonathan Ross*, *The Kumars at No.42* and *Have I Got News for You.*

Jonathan Ross was pretty much an old mate by then. He had effectively discovered Charlotte on his show five years earlier, and this year the two of them were on top form. 'God bless puberty,' Ross said when she first walked on, taking in how good she looked. Charlotte handled it all like a star – never once running out of things to say or letting his jokes get to her.

Going on *Have I Got News For You* was a hell of a lot more stressful, though. Charlotte was on Paul Merton's team and there was real pressure to be fast, funny and to know everything about current affairs, which she didn't really. She was nervous, but she looked sexy and natural and handled herself really well again. And she won people over. That's my girlfriend, I thought as each of the shows was transmitted. And after she's coming home to be with me.

Overall Charlotte and I were building up a really nice routine as our relationship put down more roots, but we were both pretty busy. Charlotte wasn't just in meetings about films, concerts and television appearances – she was trying to fit in school and had seven GCSEs to take, and in the daytime I was at college. In the evenings, as the exam dates came closer, she had revision to do and I would play suitable music and keep the kettle on while she spread her books and paperwork around the room or over the kitchen table. Once more we were just ordinary teenagers, or at least we were until Charlotte had to negotiate to sit one of her exams from LA, where her management wanted her on a promotional tour. I don't think that was a problem most other Cardiff students faced that summer, but we tried to act like it was normal.

After the exams were over we felt under a bit less pressure and knew our relationship could move up a gear. I was desperately hoping that it was time to get beyond the kissing stage.

Looking back, that first time we had got close, in her house just after we'd met, would probably have been too early. We hadn't known each other that well and so it probably wouldn't have felt so special. Now it would. Funnily enough, there was an odd link between that first near-miss and the time when we did finally make love. Back then one of the things that had stopped us was the fact that our friends had been partying downstairs. Now, at my house, we were to go ahead one night when our friends were partying upstairs.

It was summer and we were with the whole gang up in my bedroom, drinking, smoking and playing music. The skylights were open and the night was warm. I wanted Charlotte so much that night, and I desperately hoped that she wanted me. We had spent all evening just looking at each other, the way you do when you are falling in love. Everything about Charlotte was fascinating to me. The way she breathed, the way she sat, stood, moved. Her clothes, her shoes, everything was right. I couldn't take my eyes off her and I couldn't focus on anything else that was going on around me. I think everyone else knew that they were in the way, but they had nowhere else to go.

Fortunately Charlotte and I did. I whispered that she should follow me and we climbed down the staircase. Dad was away, so his big L-shaped bedroom was empty and, as usual, it was as clean as a whistle. Charlotte followed me through the door and closed it quietly behind her.

'Your dad's definitely away?' Charlotte asked as we moved towards the bed.

I nodded and we started to kiss, still standing in the middle of the room. Did I know, somehow, that this would be the night? My body and my mind were certainly hoping so.

'Come here.' I led her to the bed.

'I love you, Charlotte.'

'I love you, Stevie.'

And there it was. We had already said it in text messages and on the phone, but this was the first time we had said it face-to-face. This was the first time we could judge each other's reactions in person. I remember looking deep into Charlotte's big, wide eyes as we faced up to this milestone in our relationship. The things we both felt were at last being put into words, and once they were spoken they could never be taken away again.

In the quiet of the room, with its big windows looking up into the Cardiff night, I felt like nothing in life could ever go wrong again. It sounds soft to say it now, but that night we really did feel that we were soul mates, two people alone together, ready to take on whatever the world could throw at us. Ready to prove that love could conquer all.

Saying out loud that we loved each other would have made that particular night memorable if nothing else had happened, but we didn't stop there. I have always said that I won't embarrass Charlotte by discussing our love life in detail. I've said I will never betray her. Other people have done the dirty on Charlotte in great detail and I've always felt sorry for her and ashamed for them. Charlotte herself has even talked about our first night together, but I'm not going to go back on my word and get too intimate now.

Suffice it to say, everything seemed to happen so fast and so naturally that I can't even remember how we got our clothes off. I do remember that I could feel her skin against mine and it felt fantastic. I was kissing hard now, then I was moving my mouth and my tongue over Charlotte's face, her neck and beyond. I was trembling a bit myself and was ready to stop if she wanted me to. But I could also tell that she didn't.

I remember looking into Charlotte's eyes at one point and seeing her smile. It's such a cliché to say that time seems to stand still when you are living through moments like these. But that evening did seem to extend for so much longer than the hour or so we stayed in that room. Every minute of it seemed to be beautiful and I already knew I wanted to do it all again and again with her.

The look in Charlotte's eyes when we finally lay back on the bed showed me that she thought the same. Something good had begun and we both felt fantastic. What I found out later was that it hadn't been just me driving the action forward that night. Charlotte and Naomi had both decided that the time had come for them to lose their virginity and had made a pact to try and do it on the same night.

'It was fantastic,' Charlotte said a year later when reporters asked her about it – triggering mixed feelings in my mind. No guy is going to say he was upset to read that his girlfriend has said this about him, but I was pretty shocked that she had answered the question at all, because we had said we would always protect our privacy on things like this. Charlotte had more to say. 'Me and Naomi both got with them [me and Joshua] around the same time and we both kind of did it around the same time,' she continued. 'So it was really cool, having one of my girlfriends do it with me. It was actually on the same night. Not planned. It was just wicked to have a girlfriend there to share it all with. We were just so excited, saying, "Oh my God! I did it! What was he like? What was he like?" Some of my friends now who are virgins look at me and Naomi as the old pros.'

It wasn't, perhaps, the best phrase Charlotte could have picked, but I was glad to see that she had been so happy that night. I had always thought of it as a magical evening, and I was certainly feeling stronger about Charlotte than any other girl I had dated. I thought about her all the time, I wanted to be with her all the time and I couldn't see any reason why that should change. I realised I didn't just love her. I loved absolutely everything about her.

Unfortunately the two of us couldn't always stay alone and in love together. The rest of the world was still turning and big pressures were building up all around us. We didn't know it, but we were going to have a lot of battles to fight.

On my side the main problem was the press. It was no longer just my mobile and home phone number they were ringing. They called my family, my friends, my tutors and the other staff at college. They called neighbours, distant relatives and people from my previous schools. Everyone suddenly felt under siege and I know a lot of people really hated that feeling of being chased and bullied by people they didn't even know. There was huge pressure being put on people to talk about Charlotte and me. Money was on offer, promises of photo-shoots, work opportunities at the papers – whatever it took to persuade people to share some true or imagined gossip with reporters.

I learned the power of the simple phrase 'So, would you say that…?' Reporters would start off a conversation with those kind of words and then they would put in some words of their own and quote my friends as if it had been them who'd made the statement. It was a new world and a new experience for everyone around me and nobody was happy about it. Over time my college life was disrupted, my family were stressed and my friends were being forced to take sides. And I was still being referred to as a bad boy and a troublemaker every time my name did get in the papers.

Meanwhile Charlotte was going through her own nightmares. She was busy – finishing school, making her first film, fulfilling all her usual music commitments. And every day she seemed to be under siege from her parents, who must have wanted the unquestioning 13-year-old back rather than the confident 16-year-old who had suddenly decided she was capable of making her own decisions about life. Something had to give, and the first thing to break was Charlotte's relationship with her parents.

'Stevie, where are you? I need to come over right now.'

Charlotte called me one afternoon in the early summer when she had told her parents she was with her friend Abby. In reality she was on her way over to mine, and when she arrived she was in tears.

'I can't live there any more, Steve,' she said as she tumbled in our front door. 'I can't stay in that house. I can't put up with any more of the arguments and the stress. Please, Steve, can I move in here with you?'

I kissed her, tried to stop her crying and said yes, without a moment's hesitation.

CHAPTER SIX

SUNNY DAYS

Most people would think that a teenage multi-millionaire like Charlotte Church would dress in designer labels and carry her possessions around in designer leather bags. But the girl who was dropped off crying at my house later that day wasn't like that at all. She was wearing her usual scruffy jeans and T-shirt – clothes she would wear for days on end without washing them. And all her other kit was stuffed into big black bin-liners.

As my dad and I helped her carry everything from the car up into my bedroom, I couldn't quite believe what was happening. My beautiful girlfriend was moving in with me. It was a brilliant new adventure, but at the back of my mind was the doubt whether it was all too much too soon. I was worried about Charlotte's reasons for moving. What I wanted was for her to be here because she wanted to be with me more than anything else, but I wasn't so naive as to think that things were this simple.

Deep down I knew Charlotte was here partly as an escape. She would be very happy in this spotlessly clean house with me and my dad. But what she was really doing was moving away from her parents – and her mother in particular. People try to suggest that I used Charlotte to make a better life for myself and share in her riches and glamour. But when I look back, things were actually the other way around. Yes, Charlotte wanted to be with me, and yes we were in love. But at that point the 16-year-old girl on a tiny monthly allowance from her trust fund didn't really have anywhere else to go. My dad and I pretty much gave her a rent-free bolt-hole and that's hardly exploitation.

Charlotte's mum chose not to acknowledge this fact when she hit the media trail with a series of interviews just after Charlotte moved out. In the *Sunday Mirror* Maria admitted that they'd had a massive bust-up that had made Charlotte see red. 'One night we were in the car and we had a huge row. She said she had had enough and wanted her space. She said she was leaving and got her driver to pick her up. We thought she would be gone for a night or two and then come back to sort things out.'

Maria also said something calculated to bring back all those slurs about me being a gold-digger. 'Most 16-year-olds want to leave home at that age, but let's face it most of them can't afford it. Charlotte could and that left us completely powerless.'

Well, that's not exactly true. Apart from her allowance, Charlotte didn't actually have any real money of her own at that point. Her earnings still went into the trust fund controlled by her management. My earnings were the only ones we could really spend on a day-to-day basis. And my dad and I were the ones doing the shopping in the house, making sure the cupboards and the fridge were full. Money wasn't an issue here.

And if Maria had really wanted Charlotte back, she wasn't powerless at all. If she had known how, she could have tried being nice, for a start.

I remember Charlotte soaked in our big corner bath for much of the next day, trying to wash her problems and her worries away. I sat on the edge every now and then to ask if she was OK and if she needed anything. But I think she had all that she needed – freedom and a sense that the people closest to her were firmly on her side.

Two other men who were firmly on Charlotte's side in these difficult days were her drivers and security people, Jeff Tree and Mark Shannon. Both have said they were often torn between Charlotte and her parents, but we respected them both for choosing Charlotte that summer. I had got to know Jeff pretty well by that point, and he had brought Charlotte over with her bin-liners when she'd reached breaking point at home. He had also kept Charlotte's location secret from her mother – though he joined me in telling Charlotte that she should at least call or head home to tell her parents she was safe. This didn't actually help matters, however. Charlotte did go back to try and explain to her parents what was happening and why. But she was in tears again a couple of hours later, when she headed back through our front door.

Fortunately, life with the Johnsons managed to cheer Charlotte up pretty quick. My sisters, aunts, uncles, cousins and the neighbours were always popping round. We had to be one of the happiest houses on the street, part of a big local community where everyone knows everyone else and looks after each other. On Sunday, for example, my dad often puts a huge pot of food on the stove at about midday. The first few relatives and friends might pitch up for a chat and a bite to eat sometime after 1pm. Others will carry on coming in and out all afternoon. Sometimes there might be as many as four generations of the family all in the kitchen at the same time and I don't think Charlotte had ever seen anything quite like all this. But I do know that she loved it.

'As soon as I step through the door of Steven's home I am treated just like any other normal teenager, which is what I so desperately want to be,' she said at the time. 'His father is a real gentleman and his family is lovely.'

Charlotte also found that our house was completely different to the one described in the papers. It was summer when she first started living here, and while it isn't very big we have a fantastic suntrap at the back of the house. Double doors open on to it from the kitchen and Charlotte and I would sit there for hours some afternoons, listening to the seagulls and totally shielded from prying eyes. There's no traffic noise, no disturbances and we're right around the corner from a park, and nearby are the redeveloped docks with all its flash coffee bars, cafes and restaurants.

'Do you want to go for a walk?'

It was when we headed over to the park one sunny day that summer that Charlotte and I got our first public Posh and Becks treatment. We were holding hands, like we did almost all the time, and I put my arm round Charlotte as we stood watching some of the kids playing on the multicoloured swings and slides. It was a romantic and wonderful day, but it was about to become public property because a photographer was right there to record every frame. The pictures went on the front page of the *Sun* the following day. One of the papers that followed it up used the heading 'Angel's Delight' when introducing me, which made us both laugh.

On a more serious note, if anyone who dates someone in the public eye ever asks me for advice, one thing I would say is to wise up to just how powerful paparazzi cameras can be. I kind of thought that celebrities must always know that they are being photographed because the pictures look like close-ups.

But those huge camera lenses you see at football matches and other places mean photographers can get close-ups from a hell of a long way away. A lot of the time you don't know you are being watched – and being snapped. Once a picture has been taken, it's there forever, and even if you hate it you have to face the fact you will probably see it again and again.

The other bit of great news we got that summer came when the GCSE results were published. Charlotte had got an A in all seven subjects she'd taken – including an A* in Music, French and History. We had a great few days catching up with her old school friends that summer to celebrate or commiserate about their results. I can hardly claim I did anything to help except for making the odd cup of coffee while she was revising, but I admit I felt pretty proud that my girlfriend had done so well.

What we weren't doing at this period, when both of us were on holiday, was paying much attention to everyone else in our lives. And I think that was how one of the first big newspaper rumours about our lives took root.

REBEL CHARLOTTE LOST FOR 3 DAYS – TROUBLED STAR SPARKS POLICE HUNT screamed one of the papers, quoting all sorts of unnamed people about her supposed disappearance. So, had Charlotte ever been officially reported missing, or was it all just invented? To this day neither Charlotte nor I have any idea. We had just been hanging out with friends, with my mum and with some other relatives. There had been a lot of late nights and several days when we slept till the afternoon and didn't get out of bed till the evening. But neither of us had gone missing. Neither of us were in danger. Charlotte had just turned her phone off and wasn't getting any of her mother's messages. It was all just more time to fall in love and find out more good stuff about each other.

What I also found out was that, however hard Charlotte tries, she will probably never be the world's best cook. She is very domestic, and when we lived in our apartment together the following year she wanted us to do all our own cleaning rather than paying someone else to come in. But cooking was a different matter. Charlotte was completely fearless and would give anything a go. She would try making Thai food, spiced-up Indian food, anything we'd had in a restaurant or as a takeaway that she thought she could reproduce at home. But mostly the restaurants and takeaway places did it rather better, so in the end that's what we ate a lot more of. Especially as Charlotte burned a lot of pans and was never that keen on washing dishes.

What the two of us did spend a lot of time doing that summer was to plan what Charlotte could do next in her life. She talked about trying to get into university at some point, but didn't want to stay on in school to do A levels just yet. She had some really busy days of meetings about the film and about other commitments.

But then she would have whole stretches of time that were completely empty.

With college and my work in the music studio I had a pretty solid daily routine to follow. It was very tempting to let that slip: a whole lot of me wanted to give everything up and stay in bed with Charlotte all day – I was a typically horny male teenager, after all. But another part of me had other things I wanted to do and other places to be. I also had my dad on my back morning, noon and night, telling me that I couldn't just throw away everything I had going for me because my girlfriend's career didn't involve working regular hours.

At that point I had several jobs all at once – several of them thanks to Intech. On the music front I was starting to do some serious producing, which I loved. Putting music together was something that inspired me and I seemed to have a knack for. It was something I wanted to pursue as a career, so I was always on the lookout for new bands, musicians and singers to possibly work with. Charlotte, thankfully, was well up for going with me when I was scouting for talent or working in the studio. She knew her R&B and dance music and she was happy to fit in when we went out to listen to bands.

Charlotte wanted to shake off her own classical and operatic past and to start recording some original material of her own, so we were ideally suited to working together. We would talk and talk about the kind of tracks she should be recording, and the kind of people she should be working with. Sometimes she wanted to go the dance music route, sometimes pure R&B, sometimes hip-hop or something even harder and edgier.

We both knew crossing over was never going to be easy, though. Charlotte was famous for her big voice and her opera. That was what people thought of when they heard her name, so if she turned away from it she would turn away all her traditional fans with no guarantee that any new fans or record buyers would replace them. It was a big gamble but Charlotte was determined to follow it through. In private, behind the doors of my dad's house, she was changing fast, both as an artist and as a person. Very soon the world would be introduced to a whole new Charlotte Church.

CHAPTER SEVEN
LIVING TOGETHER

Living with Charlotte 24 hours a day was a mixture of wonderful highs and terrible lows. The highs came when it was just the two of us at home, when we were out together or having fun with friends. The lows came whenever Charlotte had to deal with her family. Then, try as I might, there was nothing I could do to make her feel any better.

Mostly we had the same sort of social life as any other teenage couple. Yes, we had occasional nights out up in London if Charlotte was going there for work and I was able to hang around and spent time with her afterwards. But apart from that we were no different to our friends Naomi and Joshua, and all the rest of our gangs of mates. We went bowling, we went to the cinema a lot, we walked around the castle grounds and talked about music and where we would like to be in a few years' time.

'Do you think they're too young?' Two friends of

ours were getting married and it was the first time Charlotte and I had ever really talked about the subject. I chose my words carefully.

'They seem to love each other. But I don't want to get married at that age.'

'So you don't think it will work out?'

'I'm not saying that. But I just think you can't really know what you want till you're in your 20s at least. It's the same with kids.'

'So what do you think our kids would look like if we ever had any?'

I looked into Charlotte's amazing eyes. 'Beautiful,' I said. Getting married and having kids would be something we would consider from our mid-20s onwards. We were getting on so well that summer, but long-term dreams like these didn't really mean very much and they certainly haven't come true. But they were nice to have.

We also spent more and more time in my recording studio at work, talking through tracks, playing around with different sounds and songs. Charlotte's main strength was lyrics and mine was music, so we actually made a pretty good team. Sometimes I would come up with melodies and Charlotte would lie around trying to catch their mood with some words or tell some kind of story. We'd sing together a bit, trying to work out if we were getting anywhere or if we needed to go back to the drawing board.

Unfortunately having so much fun when we were making music made things so much worse when we got back to the house and Charlotte's mum got on the phone. The calls had begun as soon as she had moved in and it seemed as if they would never end. Seeing Charlotte cry so much during and after those almost nightly calls just about broke my heart. Until all this began I'd thought that 'crying yourself to sleep' was just a figure of speech. Night after night with Charlotte I could see it was absolutely true.

All I could hear was Charlotte's side of the conversations, of course. But from what I could work out, and from what Charlotte used to tell me afterwards, things just seemed to go round in the same circles the way these sorts of arguments always do.

'Get out of there, get rid of him, you're ruining your life, you're throwing everything away,' was Maria's argument in a nutshell. It didn't matter how many times Charlotte screamed that she was happier than she'd ever been, that she had no intention of leaving and that it was her life anyway. Her mum just kept on with her demands, just like she had done for years. The emotional tension was equally terrible.

Maria would hurt herself, Charlotte said, if we stayed together. There were times when Charlotte really did believe that her mother might come to harm and she would have that on her conscience. I'm glad Charlotte and her mum do seem to be getting on better now, but I'll never forget how angry she was with her back then.

Funnily enough, while Charlotte's mum was on the phone every night fighting with her daughter, mine was on the phone trying to fight for her son. She and Charlotte got on fine, from the first time they met early on in our relationship. Mum was always supportive of my life and my relationships, and always wanted to know who I was seeing and hanging around with. But her woman's instincts worried that Charlotte's fame could be destructive, that neither of us knew what we were really letting ourselves in for. As time went on and the dreadful newspaper headlines began to mount up, she was particularly worried about the way the media were labelling her son and her family.

Ultimately she rang up a firm of solicitors to ask if there was any way to put the record straight and stop the papers calling me such bad things and making out I lived such a terrible life in such awful, mean streets. The reply wasn't great. It turns out there's not a lot you can do if papers want to describe your home as 'in a crime-ridden area' or to describe you as coming 'from a broken home' with all the baggage the papers know this kind of phrase will carry.

What mum was told, and what she passed on to me and my dad, was the professional opinion that the one person who could at least try and turn all this around was Charlotte. If she kept on saying how happy we were together and knocked down the rumours of me being a bad boy, then the media would eventually come around.

But the pressure from the papers had been so great, and had crept up on us so fast, that this turnaround was going to be hard to achieve. One of our next-door neighbours was quoted praising me in the papers just after Charlotte and I became a couple. 'He's not a tearaway,' Jeanette Barrett said. 'He's a lovely lad who is very kind to his mother. Charlotte's a very lucky girl.' I think I blushed reading that and probably wished she hadn't said it. But a few months later I'd changed my mind and could have done with a few more people like Jeanette to speak up for me. That said, I'm sometimes surprised that any of the neighbours still speak to me, as every time the papers mentioned me they made a point of saying what a crap part of town I came from.

'A local taxi driver joked that: "It's not a bad area but it's the kind of place where you keep a shotgun under your pillow",' said one paper when reporters first started taking pictures of my dad's house. We all wondered which bit of that being a taxi driver's *joke* had passed the reporter by, since we didn't know a single soul who owned any sort of gun, let alone felt the need to have one under their pillow.

I still don't really know why the papers took such an awful line with me. Yes, I was rude and sarcastic and swore a lot that in first conversation with the *News of the World* reporter when I thought it was just a mate winding me up. Yes, I liked to swagger around a bit and act the tough protector of my vulnerable, pretty girlfriend. And yes, I'm into music a bit harder than the *Pop Idol* songs that were topping the charts that summer.

But that doesn't make me a gangster or a criminal. What I also didn't understand was why I got linked to so many other people. One paper came up with this amazing phrase when it described my family – 'one of Steven Johnson's extended family relatives is believed to work in a South Wales massage parlour', it claimed; the implication being, I suppose, that this unknown lady was a prostitute. And then came the really heavy stuff. The stuff about my friends being murderers.

I never really knew much about all this when it happened, though I caught up fast as soon as the papers started linking me to it. It turns out that some guy followed his poor girlfriend home from work one night and shot her in her bedsit. The boyfriend was then arrested for murder and two of his mates got charged with giving him shelter and transport. As far as I was concerned, it was one of those sad stories you hear on the local news but forget about because it has nothing to do with you.

But the press went crazy. It turned out that one of the two guys charged with giving shelter might come from one of the streets near my dad's house; he might even have gone to my school. I was even 'rumoured to be friends' with him, according to one paper. And that, amazingly, was enough to link me directly to a murder. It must have made life even easier for the reporters calling me a 'bad boy' in the face of all the other evidence that suggested the opposite.

I don't like going back over all the articles, but one

example from the *Daily Mail* shows just how bad everything seemed to be getting.

'Parked outside a tiny terraced house in the back streets of Cardiff yesterday was a gleaming £40,000 BMW with a personalised number-plate: 31 SJ,' it began. 'The initials stand for Steven Johnson – a man, if that's the right word, who, it should be pointed out, is just 18. One rather obvious question springs to mind: how can a teenager (and part-time rap DJ) from a broken home in the rundown docks area of the city afford such an expensive car?'

Well, if that one 'rather obvious question' really did spring to the reporter's mind, then why didn't he ask it? Maybe he didn't have the time and decided it was easier to just write that the car was one of the 'lavish gifts' that Charlotte had given me before adding that 'she is also said to have had the vehicle insured at an annual cost of £2,000.' If the reporter had taken the time to ask his question, then Charlotte and I could have happily answered it. Charlotte would have said – as she told all the other reporters who followed up the article – that all her money is safe in her trust fund and she wouldn't be allowed to spend £2,000 on insurance, let alone £40,000 for a car. And I could have said that, yes, the car belongs to Steve Johnson. My dad, Steve Johnson. He's had the car for years and he's very proud of it. Any more obvious questions?

For so long Charlotte and I tried to laugh off the way

we were being described in the media and just get on with our lives – and I hate sounding angry about it all today. But towards the end of that summer the coverage seemed to be getting uglier and uglier and everything started to get out of control.

Back then it seemed as if we went to bed to the sound of Charlotte's mum saying she had to leave me and that terrible things would happen if she stayed. Then we woke up to see newspapers saying we were living in mean streets with danger all around.

'Should we just end it, Charlotte?' I remember asking one day after reading yet another terrible story in one of the nationals. 'Are we just ruining each other's lives by being together? Is this kind of thing ever going to end?'

Charlotte shook her head, angry at me for letting them all get to me. 'We'll sort it out,' she said, finally. 'I'll sort it out.'

A couple of days later she told me her plan. We had to get away from my dad's house, where the press were always outside the door trashing the neighbourhood. We had to prove we were a proper young couple in love. She wanted us to move into our own house together and she had got her management to sort something out. They'd picked a place in Pontcanna. But at the back of my mind it all just seemed too simple, too good to be true. Could we really get a fresh start so easily? I asked my dad for his advice and he put the fear of God in me.

'Steve, you can't move into that house,' he told me. 'They'll kill you if you do.'

'What the hell do you mean? Who's going to kill me? Nobody wants to kill me. Why would they?'

'Stevie, sit down. We need to talk.'

It turned out that my dad had been speaking to a lot of people he trusted lately and he had been hearing a lot of rumours. A couple of days earlier I had said to Charlotte that maybe I should leave her to stop us both being dragged down by all the bad publicity. Dad had heard that other people would have agreed with me. He thought that someone, somewhere, wanted me out of the picture and out of Charlotte's life. For good.

Dad reckoned I was safe living here, where I'd lived all my adult life and everyone knew everyone else. Moving to the house in Pontcanna was another story. Dad begged us not to go. He said that if we did we'd find out that the threats against me were real. He had even been told who had been approached to carry them out. Like I say, Dad knows a lot of people and they tell him things when maybe they shouldn't.

'Steve, there were some people here looking for you earlier on.'

I got a sudden chill the next day when I walked into the Intech offices and got that message. The people hadn't said what they wanted, who they were or if they would be back. It could have been mates, it could have been work people, it could have been reporters. Or it could have been something more sinister. Everyone was jumpy and nothing felt safe any more.

I remember lying awake in bed that night, Charlotte by my side. Could this sort of stuff really be true? It was like some episode from a mafia film or a television show. Do hit men really exist outside of fiction? All I knew that night was that, yes, criminals and guns exist and that bad things do happen. I knew that people seemed to see me as a massive problem in Charlotte's life. That a lot of money was swilling around Charlotte's career and that a lot of people wanted to make sure she didn't start making her own decisions and her own music.

Whether that all added up to a clear and present danger I don't know. Neither did Charlotte when I told her about it the next day. Then, more than ever, we felt totally under siege from the world. It seemed like no one would allow us to just have ordinary lives together, that everyone everywhere wanted to split us up. In a strange way, realising that actually pulled us even closer together. If a relationship is too easy, then maybe you never really get close. When you are constantly hitting difficulties, you dig deeper and fight harder to make things work. Charlotte and I decided that we would not give in to everyone else. And we were going to live in our own house together.

Pontcanna is one of the nicest parts of Cardiff, full of cafes, shops and restaurants. A teenage couple getting their first house together there should be blissfully happy. It should almost have been a 'carrying over the threshold' moment when we first arrived. But for all our bravado we had both been spooked by all the rumours, and we were actually pretty scared about what might happen now we were away from my dad's. Neither of us slept very well on any of the nights we spent in Pontcanna. The place seemed tainted from the start and, while the rent had been paid for almost a year, we moved back to my dad's within a week.

The threats to our lives turned to nothing, but that's not to say they weren't real at the time. We had certainly thought that they were, and it took a long time to recover from them. In the end, we decided the best thing was to take our time and plan a new home of our own later in the year, rather than relying on others to do it for us. That way we could stay in control and feel more secure.

Throughout this period we were also getting ready for another brief separation. Charlotte was going to Los Angeles for a big bash and a series of meetings with her record company, Sony. It would only be for three days but it would seem like far longer.

'Come with me, Steve.'

It was the request I had dreaded. On one hand I really wanted to go. It would mean we didn't get separated, and a trip to LA would be pretty cool. But I had learned a bit about how the media worked, and I knew that if I went I'd come in for yet another attack. They'd already turned things around and called me a leech when Charlotte had been living in my family home. They'd go into overdrive if I lived in her hotel room for a few days. So I knew it was too early to go on one of Charlotte's work trips. There would be other times, I said. Times when the pressure wasn't on and we wouldn't have to worry about what the papers would say about us.

Little did we know the papers couldn't have said anything worse about me going with Charlotte than they did about me staying at home. The classic *News of the World* sting was about to begin, and I never even saw it coming.

CHAPTER EIGHT

THE STING

It was September 2002 and with Charlotte away I was hanging out with my mates, kicking back and having some fun. Then my mobile rang. It's the same phrase that caught me out back when I had been first seeing Charlotte, and it was going to cause nothing but trouble all over again.

'Hello Steven, I'm from the *News of the World*.'

This time, fortunately, I knew enough to believe that he was who he said he was and that it wasn't someone from college trying to wind me up. 'We're in Cardiff and we want to run a story about you and Charlotte. Can you come over and meet us so we can talk it over with you?'

I looked around. I couldn't really, because I was with my friends, we were having a good time and I didn't have anything I wanted to say to anyone from the papers. So that's what I said and it turned out that wasn't a problem. You can all come over. We've got a couple of rooms, we can have some drinks. It'll be fun, the reporter said. I put my hand over the phone, told my mates who it was and what they wanted and asked what everyone wanted to do. Obviously everyone wanted to head over there. What group of bored teenagers wouldn't take up the chance to hang out in a flash hotel for a while when someone else was picking up the tab? It all seemed like a bit of a laugh, so off we went to the St David's Hotel a few streets away by the seafront.

There were two reporters there when we arrived and they couldn't have been chummier or nicer. Nothing was too much trouble for them, nothing was off-limits, the booze could run freely and it was all going to be just a relaxed, cool chat. I know my mates were pretty impressed by the whole thing and I felt pretty cool being the one that was introducing them to this kind of life and these kind of people. I wanted to milk the situation for all it was worth and show them just how media-savvy and worldly I had become. I'd play the reporters' games, say what they wanted me to say and take control of the whole situation. Like I say, it was a laugh.

The whole thing went on for hours and hours and, of course, all the reporters wanted to talk about was Charlotte. And sex. I'm not a prude. I've got a lot of bravado and I like to show off in front of my mates, but I've never been happy about talking about sex in front of strangers. So I said I'd only carry on the conversation if they paid me £100,000.

Will anyone ever believe me when I say I was only joking? I hope they will, for three main reasons. One, because to this day I have never given any details of my sex life with Charlotte. Two, because Charlotte believed me and she knows me better than anyone. And three, because the way the whole story ultimately got reported was so full of holes that it should never have been taken seriously.

The first thing in my favour was the fact that the *News of the World* realised I wasn't actually going to betray Charlotte in any way. They had no story. And so the weeks passed and they had nothing to publish. Other papers, somehow, took a different view. Don't ask me how, but maybe some *Daily Mirror* reporter was one day speaking to a *News of the World* reporter and decided to run with a second-hand version of events which never really happened in the first place.

'The boyfriend of schoolgirl singing star Charlotte Church is trying to sell the story of their seven-month fling for £50,000,' it began. 'Steven Johnson, 18, waited for Charlotte to fly off to Los Angeles before contacting newspapers and magazines – fuelling rumours that she had dumped him and he was cashing in,' it continued. But I hadn't contacted any newspapers or magazines. The *News of the World* had rung me. And Charlotte hadn't dumped me and I wasn't cashing in – as far as I was aware there weren't even any rumours that our relationship was in trouble.

'Johnson, who refused to confirm he had split with

16-year-old Charlotte, said his story contained sensational details about his romance with the millionaire soprano.' Well, I would have refused to confirm that I had split with Charlotte because we hadn't. Finally the paper got something right.

'Johnson took over two rooms in a five-star hotel in Cardiff as he hawked his story around. The hotel is a mile from his father's home, which the young couple used as a meeting place.' Well, no again. I didn't take over two rooms in a five-star hotel. I was invited to a five-star hotel. And Charlotte and I didn't use Dad's home as some seedy-sounding 'meeting place'. We lived there. Very happily, thank you very much.

The article went on and on. My friends and I 'knocked back £40 bottles of champagne and shots of Jack Daniel's during six hours of negotiations,' it said, skating over the fact that all we had done was drink what we had been offered without ever being shown any price tags. Yes, we probably did make a bit of noise and joke about wanting to watch soft-core porn on the hotel television and stuff like that. We were there for a long time and we were teenagers having a laugh, after all.

Other papers tried to hint at other, darker things. 'Johnson and his cronies were giggling and lethargic, said one of those present in the hotel room that day. They did not smoke drugs in the room but left several times to stand on the balcony,' wrote one. Well, what is all that about, exactly? If they had something to say, then they should surely have the guts to say it. Or did they know the allegations just weren't true?

Finally there was the line that I said a magazine had offered me £100,000 for my story and some photographs. If it was true that I wanted money, and that a magazine had offered me that much for the story, then why wouldn't I have accepted it? Why would I be there with other people, trying – as they said in the massive headline – to sell the same story for just £50,000? Nothing added up. The only truth I could see on the whole page was that poor Charlotte was in Los Angeles and that this could break her heart.

'Charlotte, I've screwed up. And I've been screwed.'

That was the only way I could describe it to her on the phone. But, of course, her family had already been on to her to crow about my supposed betrayal. They were with her in LA, desperate to tell her that they had been right all along; that this was final proof that I was a bad guy, trouble, a loser and that she should come straight home to them when they all got back to Cardiff.

Charlotte, my girlfriend, listened to my side of the story, however. She knows me. She knows the press. She knows the business. And when she came back from LA she came straight home to me. I remember hugging her very, very tightly that night. When you think someone is about to be snatched away from you forever, you realise just how much you want them.

When you think you've lost them you can't let go the next time you see them.

'If only it was just us. If only it weren't for everyone else. Why does everyone want to split us up?' I asked when we had gone over and over the events of the past few days. 'Why can't things be normal for us?'

We stayed close that whole night, and long into the next morning. Charlotte was jet-lagged and a bit woozy and we had spent a lot of time talking the previous night. But she knew she was home and that our relationship was sound. We were sure we could tough this one out together like all the others. What got to me most over the next few weeks was the fact that the papers had decided to move on from attacking me. They had decided it was time to attack Charlotte instead, and this time they got really ugly.

'Charlotte the rebel may be going off the rails' decided the *Daily Mirror* one slow news day in October 2002 when they tracked down what they called 'a behavioural expert' to give some opinions on Charlotte, a girl she had never met. And so it went on. All the papers jumped on the bandwagon, saying Charlotte was throwing her career and her life away, that she was risking everything, spiralling out of control. 'The voice of an angel is on the road to hell' was one of the few lines in all this coverage that we laughed at together because it was actually pretty neat. Everything else was rubbish.

One other pressure was building up at that point as

well. Charlotte's mother had come up with a new strategy to split us up. First of all she was trying to persuade her 16-year-old daughter to move 150 miles away to London, where she hoped she might meet and date the fellow celebrities Maria seemed to be obsessed with. Then, when Charlotte kept on telling her that she was happy in Cardiff with me, her mates and all the people and places she knew, Maria upped the stakes. She said Charlotte should move thousands of miles away to America for the sake of her career.

If all you care about is selling records, signing deals and filling stadiums, then a move to LA would have made sense. Over there Charlotte could have spent all her time with the movers and shakers in the industry, schmoozing middle-aged executives, planning PR stunts, turning herself into some sort of global brand. She could have focused 100 per cent on her career, cut herself off from her past and, of course, left me behind.

But at 16, those were not Charlotte's dreams. We spent enough time laughing about some of the dull meetings she had to sit through as it was. The last thing she wanted was to turn that into a full-time existence. She had already lost the first half of her teenage years to work. She wasn't up to lose the second half as well.

That's not to say that Charlotte didn't put the hours in for work once her GCSEs were out of the way. Nor is it to say that all this work was boring or unsatisfying.

She had her fair share of fun invites and good times, and her working life seemed to dovetail pretty well with mine. Our main strategy, whatever we did in the daytime, was to make sure that we ended every night together, however late that might be.

One time Charlotte had sung at a charity evening and then gone to a perfume launch sponsored by Christian Dior, where the freebies on offer were supposed to be brilliant. Meanwhile I had been working late at the studio and had then gone to see some musicians my business partners and I were thinking of working with. Charlotte and I kept on sending texts to each other as the night went on, just as we always did. Then, when her evening and mine were both over, we arranged to meet up in Creation nightclub in town. Charlotte had some other friends with her still and I remember holding her handbag for most of the night while she danced with them all. I was with my girlfriend, and I liked it. She was happy dancing, so I was happy just being there, drinking in the atmosphere and chatting to whoever else was around – and knowing that we were going to be heading home together when the lights went up.

When we got home we went through our usual late-night routine. Kettle on, bit of toast, chilling out on the sofa and talking about our days.

Most nights both of us stank of cigarette smoke, the big downside of spending all night at gigs and clubs. But it didn't really matter because both of us had been smoking a little bit as well. And that was set to trigger the biggest media storm yet; one that would make it even harder for us to stay together, and one which would add yet one more name to the list of people trying to split us up. That name was Steve Johnson. My dad.

CHAPTER NINE

THE SMOKING GIRL

Ask my dad what his first impression of Charlotte was and he'll probably say one word: 'suspicious'. He didn't like her mother and he didn't want a mini-version of Maria in his house dating his son. But Dad wasn't going to stereotype people and judge them without knowing them. So Charlotte got the benefit of the doubt and after a long, long time she won him over. She got to use his nickname, George, and I think she was always completely comfortable hanging around the house with him whether I was there or not.

Early on he told her that she should treat the place like it was hers – that she could bring her friends round and relax there even when I was out. So after a while it became more than just a second home to her; it was her real home and the three of us couldn't have been happier. Charlotte's mum and the media might have been trying to pull us apart outside the front door but inside it everything was cool. Or at least it was until that one October morning when Charlotte headed outside with a cigarette in her hand.

Mention this incident to my dad and to this day he gets so angry he can hardly get the words out fast enough. He had been really suffering from all the bad press about the kind of house Charlotte and I were supposed to be living in. The papers constantly said that our street was in 'the centre of one of Cardiff's most crime-ridden estates' – really pissing off any of the neighbours who wanted to sell their homes or just feel good about where they lived. As if that wasn't bad enough, reporters would even call our house itself 'run-down' or worse – even though they had never been through the front door and could see through the windows that it was modern, well maintained and as spotlessly clean as any you could find on millionaire's row. Dad was also worried about all the references to the area being full of drug dealers, as he feared people would think that sort of thing might go on under his roof – something he would never have allowed.

The smoking incident happened at a time when interest in Charlotte and I seemed to be at fever pitch. Groups of photographers and reporters stood outside our house all day and half the night, and because we only have a small front yard they were literally just a matter of feet from our living-room windows. They spent their time mainly chatting, talking on mobile phones, smoking and sitting on the bonnets of their cars. I still can't believe it makes sense for them to wait for so-called celebrities in this way.

'Go on, it'll be a laugh. Put a hood on and go out there pretending to be me.' Charlotte was always ready to have some fun winding up the photographers with my sisters. When we tried to fool them like this they would all leap into action as if they had been stung – desperate not to miss a thing in case it really was Charlotte and I coming into view. Then we would watch them slump back for another long boring wait when they realised we were staying put.

'Smoking's not good for you. It'll kill your voice even if it doesn't kill you.'

No one in my house ever thought it was a good idea for Charlotte to be smoking, at any time. That has to be bad for your throat and your voice, and when, like Charlotte, your voice is your fortune you would think that you would want to look after it. Some singers refuse to perform their shows if people smoke in the venue – in case the smoke affects their vocal cords. Charlotte, however, was often so unhappy with her professional life and all the pressures that it put on her that she did seem prepared to risk it, so she lit up among her friends and happily smoked in front of me and my dad. What she had been so careful never to do, however, was to smoke in front of the press.

'OK, I'm ready. Let's go.' She grabbed her bag that afternoon as we got ready to head out to meet some friends. And she had a newly lit cigarette in her hand.

'There's photographers out there, remember,' my dad said to her from the living room, pointing to the cigarette. But she just shrugged, swore about the snappers and headed towards the door. At first, Dad wasn't prepared to let her go.

'Charlotte, if you go out holding that, they'll crucify us,' he said, standing up.

Another shrug and Charlotte moved towards the door.

'This is my house, they'll get pictures of you outside my house. Finish it or put it out, Charlotte.' But she didn't. We headed outside and, as my dad had known, the photographers went wild, crowding us out and firing off what sounded like rolls of film as we headed down the street. The *Sun* put the shot on the front page, and every other paper followed up on it. Could we have given the papers any more ammunition to depict me as the ultimate bad boy helping to ruin his perfect girlfriend's life? The reports over the next few days and weeks were back feeding on the downward spiral Charlotte's life was now supposed to be on. And how I, my deadbeat family and our terrible living conditions were supposed to be behind it all. My favourite description was the paper that said Charlotte had been seen smoking 'outside an ordinary terraced house'. As opposed to what, we wondered with a chuckle. Other papers made it harder to laugh, however.

'Charlotte the scruff has a puff' led *The Sun*, having a dig at her clothes as well. 'Charlotte the scruffy smoker ignites new row over boyfriend' said the

Daily Mail, bringing it back to me again. Reporters hinted, wrongly, that Charlotte's cigarette had been cannabis, and did another massive ring-around of our friends and contacts to try and find proof that we were taking drugs.

, A bit later on they had another go when they got a picture of Charlotte on my arm and wearing a pair of cute little palm-tree earrings that she had just bought at Top Shop. So how did a picture like that create a storm? Because the papers wrote that they were actually shaped like cannabis leaves and that she had bought them in some dodgy, druggy market. After that the hints, suggestions and inventions went on.

'Steven had no money and no morals, a drug habit and "friends" involved in a murder case. How, to her family's despair, he's snared angel-voiced star Charlotte Church and turned her into a cigarette-smoking rebel', the *Daily Mail* screamed one day above the same-old FALLEN ANGEL headline the papers had been using for months. Throw in some bizarre story that popped up saying Charlotte and I had secretly recorded a dance track called 'Stick it in Cider' as part of a bid to find her a new adult audience and the madness was complete.

Oddly enough, at this point, when even my dad had joined the people saying Charlotte and I were wrong for each other, her dad suddenly came out with a little bit of support. 'I'm not worried about my daughter. Why should I be? She's entitled to a private life,' he said when everyone else was laying into her about the cigarettes. Some days it felt as if the whole world was upside down and Charlotte and I had no idea where to turn for support or where the next attack might come from. So we retreated back into our own lives, relying on our own company.

Charlotte, though, was determined to try and give us a fresh start and to get rid of some of the worst pressures in her life in the process. She wanted to put the record straight about her actions and to go it alone with her career. And that meant taking on the media and taking control away from her mother.

Her big media battle began with an interview with Des O'Connor, where she partly embarrassed me and partly made me happy by calling me 'really, really lovely, really sweet'. I'd gone from the hard-man bad boy to a big girl's blouse in one big leap. But I knew that was for the best. The big one, however was a last-minute BBC appearance on *Parkinson* on 23 November. Charlotte was nervous, of course, but the Parkinson people were dead nice in the run-up to the show and were happy to talk through how the recording was likely to go, which took some of the pressure off.

Charlotte spent ages trying to work out what to wear. She wanted to look grown up to show viewers how much she had changed in recent years. She wanted to look good. But she had also laid into some other female singers lately for looking too tarty, so she had to tread carefully. In the end we settled on a white jacket and trousers with a great, low-cut, black top which showed just enough cleavage to match all the messages she wanted to get across. She was wearing one of her favourite new necklaces, had her hair straightened and glossed up and I knew she would knock them all dead with that look.

I'll never forget the first time I saw Charlotte scrubbed up for a photo-shoot back in the spring. She had been doing an exclusive interview for some magazine and I stood open-mouthed when she came out of the stylist's chair and headed in front of the cameras. I had always loved her skin and her eyes – even first thing in the morning, when she wasn't wearing any make-up at all. But that day she simply took my breath away. The make-up people had turned her into the kind of person you wouldn't think could possibly exist – they had made her some sort of goddess and I could see why so many people she had never met had fallen in love with her.

Anyway, she and Parkinson got talking about the way the papers had started to treat her. Charlotte hit some of the press lies on the head straightaway – including the fact that she hadn't, of course, bought me or insured me a £40,000 BMW because she didn't have access to any money apart from her weekly allowance. Hopefully that will make some of the papers feel pretty stupid, I thought, not knowing that this kind of thing didn't bother them at all.

'I'm only young, but it is the strongest I have ever felt,' she then said when Parky asked about our relationship. 'He's really lovely and we get on really well. The stories that he's a bad boy and he does this and he does that are just not true.' Then, at last, the truth about the *News of the World* sting. 'I don't believe he did that,' she interrupted when Parky started talking about it. 'Nobody else knows him. I know him well, and I just think the press say things to make someone react. I know all his family and they seem like really nice people so I just don't believe it.'

The rest of their chat took in the smoking incident, and how she knew that getting addicted could damage her voice so she had decided to try and stop. Then they got on to her relationship with her mother and Charlotte came out with some stuff about how close they had always been since childhood but how much she wanted more independence now she was an adult. Overall she looked and sounded good, gave a great performance of 'Bridge over Troubled Water' and got some decent publicity for her greatest-hits album, which was also what the whole thing was about.

Did I want her to say more about me and make it clearer that I wasn't the bad guy I was always painted as? Yes I did, even though I had blushed at the way she had described me to Des O'Connor. And my mum, dad and sisters certainly did want a bit more of that with Parkinson. But at least it was a start, I thought, and it certainly couldn't have made matters worse.

Just before the Parkinson show, Charlotte had tried unsuccessfully to shake her career free from her mother's influence. That task was never going to be easy so Charlotte had been spending a lot of time speaking to her record company, PR people, all sorts of advisers and insiders about where she wanted to go and how she could get there. She wasn't complaining about any of the work that had been done for her career so far. She knew that she had needed a lot of guidance when she'd been 13 and carving out a career as a child star in the world of classical music and opera.

But now, like any teenager, she wasn't sure that older people would really understand the new career she was aiming for or that they would be able to book her into the right venues and find her the right deals. Moving on and taking control away from her mother was really just one more part of growing up, but after the way the last few months of Charlotte's life had been reported we were ready for some fireworks when this news came out. Sure enough, 'Charlotte sacks her own mother' seemed to be the most common interpretation, which suited me pretty well but ultimately started to spook Charlotte.

'I don't hate my mum and I don't want to stab her in the back,' she told me when we sat at home reading the papers and looking at what was being written on the internet about it all. Charlotte just wanted her mum to accept that I was in her daughter's life for good and to try and get along with me. All their problems, and all their late-night rows on the telephone, came down to that and she didn't like the fact that her mum was now being called a bad manager. Charlotte could put up with endless personal insults, but she knew how damaging professional ones could be so she got on the phone to try some damage limitation.

The official statement that she finally came up with and released seemed to get buried and was pretty much ignored, as these things are. But, for the record, it said: 'My mother remains very involved in my career but obviously on a different level due to my growing independence and own experience. Now that I have completed my studies, everyone is in agreement that it is the appropriate time for me to embark upon my US tour with my management and tour staff.'

The key fact in this statement was that, for the first time in Charlotte's life, her mum and dad were to be left behind in Wales when she went on tour overseas. It was a big, important tour as well – 15 key dates across North America in the run-up to Christmas, which is the biggest record-buying time of the year. There was a lot at stake and everyone was nervous. Which was why Charlotte wanted me to come with her.

'Please, Steve. It'll be an adventure. And I can't do it on my own.'

I should have gone. It was just like last time, though, when she had wanted me to go to LA with her for the big bash Sony had thrown for her. We could have been together, we could have had a laugh, we could have escaped all the pressures and the press in the UK for a while and found some freedom for a change. As a gentleman I should also have agreed to go because

Charlotte was nervous and scared and looked like she needed my support. She was making a brave move, striking out on her own and it would be lonely on the road, with only the older tour bosses for company. Plus, of course, I always got a buzz out of seeing Charlotte sing. Her kind of music wasn't my kind at all, but I love any form of live performance and I know talent when I hear it.

'Look, you know the papers will crucify me if I go with you. And your mum will go mad.'

'Screw the papers. And I'll sort it with my mum. What's the point of us being together if we keep giving in and staying apart?'

All I could say was that I would think about it, and I did. But I also thought about the way the press would treat it and about my work back at home. My dad had calmed down a bit after the cigarette incident, but he was still pretty down on the way my relationship with Charlotte could affect my future. He kept on telling me I needed to get serious about building up a career and an income of my own, and my disappearing to America for three weeks wouldn't make for happy families. So in the end I knew I had to say no to Charlotte. Unfortunately that wasn't easy, either, because as the big tour approached she had started to come down with a massive cold, an ear infection and she was starting to feel even more vulnerable than ever. Those were not good days in the Johnson house.

Saying goodbye to the person you love for three

weeks is never easy. But for us it was harder because of all the issues of whether or not we needed to be separated at all. Charlotte kept saying it would never be too late for me to change my mind – that they could get me an extra seat on the plane right up until the last minute and that I didn't even need to pack because we could buy anything I needed to wear when we got to America. And I kept saying that I had to stay at home.

That's where I was when Charlotte arrived at Gatwick Airport for her plane to Atlanta, where she had been asked to switch on the Christmas lights before the start of the tour. We had been speaking on the phone on and off for most of her car journey there. Some of the time she sounded like the old Charlotte – excited, confident, ready to face live audiences and get through some new challenges. Other times she just sounded tired, ill and fed up.

For some reason our conversations went back to all the old issues that people had always tried to stir up. We were both aware that the last time she'd gone to America and I'd stayed at home, my bravado had got me plastered all over the newspapers and called a love rat and worse. This time I told her reporters could invite me, all my friends, my whole family and the entire population of Cardiff to a posh hotel for vintage champagne, but I wouldn't fall for the same scam twice.

On the personal front Charlotte and I had other rumours to face down. 'I'm faithful to you, Charlotte and I always will be,' I said again and again on the phone that day. 'I'll never do anything apart from flirt with another girl while you're away.' I should have known that making a joke like that would only have made matters worse.

In the background Charlotte had other issues to face as well. When she wasn't on the phone to me on that car journey she was on the phone to her mum and dad, who, no doubt, were worried about their daughter heading off on such a big trip on her own. For someone who wasn't feeling 100 per cent, the pressure was high.

The last time we spoke was when Charlotte was leaving the VIP lounge at Gatwick to board her flight. Her cold and her ear problem were getting worse and she was in a really bad state. The next day the papers would say that she had had a 'tantrum' on the way to the plane and had refused to go any further. Would you want to go through a long transatlantic flight if you felt ill, photographers were chasing you and the whole world seemed out to get you? Charlotte had the chance to head back home for some love, attention and rest instead, so I don't blame her for taking it.

She also had several days to go before rehearsals started for the tour, let alone the tour itself. So the idea that she was 'facing the biggest crisis of her short career and may face multimillion pound legal action' (as one tabloid put it) was pretty ridiculous.

Anyway I didn't actually know a thing about all this until the front door to the house banged open and Charlotte rushed up the stairs to my room. She hadn't called to say she had refused to fly or that she was coming back to Cardiff.

'Steve, I couldn't go.'

'I don't believe it.'

'I just had to see you.'

'Charl, come here.'

We held each other close again while I tried to work out if she was OK. She was breathing deeply, not just because of the two flights of stairs. Our world was closing in on us again and it felt as if all we had was each other to fight it.

Over in another part of Cardiff, Charlotte's PR people were working overtime to try and sort things out. Part of their job was to hit back at the ever-growing stories of a rift between Charlotte and her mother. What they wanted was pictures of the pair laughing, joking and getting on well to calm down the American paymasters. But no such pictures had been taken for months – you can draw your own conclusions from that – so a stage-managed set of pictures of Charlotte and Maria was organised. It would remain the only set of photos of them available for some time, and you can draw your own conclusions from that as well.

Still feeling weak from her illness, Charlotte finally gave in and agreed that her mother could come to America with her after all. The not-so-happy family flew off at the weekend. These three extra days with Charlotte would make a dent in the three weeks before we saw each other again. That, at least, felt better. And surely nothing could go wrong with the tour now?

Charlotte and I spoke on the phone at least once a day while she was away and it turned out things weren't that easy from the start. The tour was called 'A Royal Christmas' and co-starred Julie Andrews and Christopher Plummer from *The Sound of Music*. The first night was in Cincinnati, and reading the coverage back in Britain, I got another lesson in how the press can twist any 'facts' to suit their agendas.

The previous week, for example, the *Daily Mail* had declared that the concerts were 'sell-outs' because it wanted to whip up a storm about them possibly being cancelled with huge legal liabilities if Charlotte didn't get to America in time. Now the same paper said 'she walked on stage in a stadium littered with empty seats' and that 'barely a third of the 12,000 seats were sold in the US Bank Arena, in spite of a wealth of hype and a well co-ordinated publicity campaign. At one point the audience was encouraged to move into huge banks of unsold seats, priced at up to £65, to create the illusion that the stadium was fuller than it was.'

Well, they can't have it both ways. Only in newspaper-land can a concert be both a sell-out and two-thirds empty at the same time. And this wasn't the only bad coverage Charlotte was to get that week. The next rumour was totally unbelievable, hurtful and massively cruel.

'After the show she threw a tantrum and refused to

meet a group of relatives of cast members who had been waiting patiently backstage to see her. "Fuck this," she was heard to snap at her embarrassed entourage. "I didn't agree to no meet and greet. Hello!" The waiting party included a handicapped child and the wheelchair-bound mother of Royal Philharmonic conductor Sir George Daugherty. The singer then walked out to board her luxury tour bus and it was left to concert co-host Dame Julie Andrews to welcome the group and sign autographs.'

Bad enough for you? Well, more of the same followed. 'The singer is not exactly flavour of the month among tour staff either,' the paper went on. 'They have started to bicker over the teenager's increasingly diva-esque demands which include chocolate cake and Italian ham in her dressing room. One said: "She's the worst I've ever seen. It's not as if this is a sell-out event that justifies that sort of treatment."' Oh, and the paper said Christopher Plummer was pissed off with Charlotte as well for supposedly keeping him waiting for the final rehearsal before the show.

Nothing in those articles was describing the Charlotte Church I knew. The idea of Charlotte throwing a fit and refusing to meet any fans, let alone disabled fans or children, was totally out of order. The whole time we had been together, whether we were at a fancy work do or just shopping locally for groceries, fans would come up to Charlotte. Sometimes they just wanted to say hello, sometimes to shake her hand, sometimes to ask for one (or several) autographs. And quite often, especially as mobile phones started to get cameras, they wanted to be photographed next to her.

If you're shopping for groceries and toiletries you're probably not going to be over the moon about having your picture taken. But I can put my hand on my heart and say that Charlotte never flinched, never snubbed anyone and was never rude. She might be tired, she might want privacy, but she knew that the public had made her rich and famous and that she had to always give something back. I was always impressed by that, even if it did mean me standing waiting time after time when she had to talk to her fans.

Charlotte was a real professional. And if she acted like that when she was off duty on the streets and in the pubs, clubs and shops of Cardiff, then she would certainly act like that after a concert in America when she would see herself as in full work mode. 'I didn't agree to no meet and greet. Hello!' No way. There was no way I would believe that she had said that. I also knew she would be devastated to read it.

We had spoken on the phone after that first Cincinnati concert and everything had been cool. Charlotte was pretty knackered, and she had been a bit pissed off because there had been some technical problems in the hall with some of the microphones. And yes, it hadn't been sold out. But it was still nearly four weeks till Christmas, so maybe you can't expect a

Christmas concert to be the most popular show in town. She said the management were telling them that sales for later in the run were far better – and she didn't seemed worried about it at all. She said Julie Andrews and Christopher Plummer were nice, the orchestra was good and all the behind-the-scenes staff were cool. She also seemed to be getting on a bit better with her mother and said that both of them were making a massive effort to just enjoy the moment and act like they used to do, rather than talk about or focus on all their long-term issues. She'd also been round to one of Rod Stewart's house parties and met Shaquille O'Neal. I told her it all sounded brilliant and that I missed her.

So reading that one report on the same concert a day or so later came as a complete shock.

'Why, why, why do they write these things? Why do they want to destroy me?' I tried to comfort Charlotte after she was told about the article on the next date of her tour. Part of me felt a little bit guilty, a little bit responsible, because as usual my name had been dragged into it. 'It is clear that the difficulties created by Miss Church's romance with rap DJ Steven Johnson, 18, are still troubling her,' it had said, without backing this up in any way or explaining quite why it thought I was to blame for these events they suggested had happened on the other side of the Atlantic.

At one point, reading another article saying what an ungrateful, unfriendly bitch Charlotte was, it crossed my mind that maybe I should walk away from her.

Maybe Charlotte and I couldn't face up to all this and fight it out after all. Maybe it would be better for us both if we split up so she could carry on with her career as she had done before. The pressure to do so seemed to be getting higher all the time and being together seemed to bring us nothing but trouble.

But then Charlotte said that she missed me, that she had seen some stuff that day that would have made me laugh and that she wished I had been there to see it too. Despite the distance, we still felt completely connected, and straight away I knew we had to stay strong and stay together.

Over the next couple of days Charlotte called to tell me about the way the American newspapers were treating the tour and the Cincinnati incident. Pretty much the only American newspaper that I had ever heard of was the *National Enquirer*, which had once run the 'Rainbow Family' story on the Johnsons but was now notorious for its ludicrous stories about finding Elvis on the moon. I dreaded to think what they might be making up about Charlotte.

As it turned out they weren't doing anything like that. Charlotte read out some of the local reports from Michigan, where she had gone after Cincinnati. The papers there had actually done some research. They had spoken to people at the previous concert, and they had been there when some competition winners and well-wishers had been taken to Charlotte's dressing room for a very happy and very relaxed 'meet and greet' after her next few shows. Charlotte, they discovered, was as charming and as willing to meet her fans as any star they had interviewed. The British claims, they said, were totally untrue.

It was 1–0 to Charlotte, at last. A big fat zero for the absurdities that had been printed about her in Britain. We ended that phone conversation a little bit happier than the last one. And every day that went past brought her return date that little bit closer. It was finally starting to feel a bit like Christmas.

CHAPTER TEN
TIME TO PARTY

I got the call just after 8am, just after Charlotte's plane landed back in Britain on 23 December. She was on her way home and all I wanted to do was see her and hold her. It takes a couple of hours to get from London to Cardiff by car, so taking into account the time it would take to get through customs and get her luggage, I reckoned she would be here around about midday.

I also knew her mother would be in the Mercedes with her, so I wasn't sure exactly how the evening was going to work out. Charlotte had said on the phone that she and her mum had probably done well to spend so much time together on the tour. They had built some bridges and managed to talk without shouting, screaming or starting to cry. It was quite a turnaround, but I was pretty certain that things hadn't been patched up well enough for Maria to pop round for a cup of tea and to show the Johnsons their holiday snaps that afternoon.

'Hello, gorgeous.'

'God, I missed you.'

That first hug when Charlotte's driver finally dropped her off at mine was fantastic. Charlotte was tired, of course, but those big green eyes were as alive and happy as ever when she flopped down on the leather sofa in our living room. That evening one of the first things Charlotte did was to have another long, hot bath. Dad had put big skylights into our bathroom roof when he had rebuilt the house, and Charlotte and I would light candles in there and gaze up through the steam into the night. When planes passed overhead we used to joke about what the papers would say if a pilot ever had a zoom lens and a steady hand as he headed into Cardiff Airport.

What we also had to do was sort out what was going to happen over Christmas. Like any couple in love, we wanted to wake up together on Christmas morning, hoping it would be the first of many. I suppose we were hardly alone in finding the bit after that rather difficult to arrange. Loads of couples have divided loyalties at Christmas, even if their two families get on well. So, like everyone else, we decided to compromise and split the day between our two houses. Charlotte had lunch and opened her presents at her mum and dad's without me and then headed back to mine to join all the kids and the fun here for a long, lazy dinner that night. At least our families lived pretty close to each other.

Charlotte and I had agreed we wouldn't go crazy on

the present front – restricting ourselves to just a few small parcels. I got Charlotte some of her favourite perfume, and she bought me a sweatshirt. It was nice, ordinary stuff, and it kept us feeling just like every other pair of loved-up teenagers across the country. I've never normally liked that week between Christmas and New Year because it always feels empty and endless. But with Charlotte it just felt perfect. We didn't have any work or other pressures on us. So we just caught up on our DVDs in bed, ate what we liked when we liked, and did a lot of extra sleeping. It was like a holiday and it just felt brilliant.

'What a bloody amazing year it's been,' I said to Charlotte on New Year's Eve as we got ready to head out for a big night out with our mates. She said exactly the same thing to me the next night when we lay on the bed making plans for 2003 and looking back on everything we had done together so far.

All the walls of my room are white, and one night ages ago Charlotte had written, 'I love Charlotte more than anything else in the world' in red paint on the brickwork above the chimney breast in front of the bed. 'Just to make sure you don't forget,' she had said afterwards. Those words flickered in the candlelight that New Year night. And they were right – I did.

We worked out that night that we had already survived two families that really disliked each other. Two parents on her side who seemed to hate me. Newspaper reporters who wanted to split us up and make out Charlotte's career was over. We had survived separations, busy days and tearful nights. None of that had been any fun but suddenly, lying in bed together where we were always happy, it was possible to see the positive side. It had, surely, made us stronger. For all the bad news in public we were still incredibly happy when we were alone together or out with friends in private. We were looking forward to 2003. There was masses we still wanted to do together.

First up we decided that we might as well say 'to hell with the criticism' and enjoy the good life. Charlotte got invited to some great bashes, but up until now I had shied away from going to any of them with her because I thought I would just get called a parasite or a hanger-on. But as the papers just attacked me anyway, it seemed I had nothing to lose by spending more time with my girlfriend. Our New Year's resolution for 2003 was simple: we were going to have a lot more fun.

What Charlotte and I also had at the start of that year was a secret. Later that month Charlotte was going to release her first adult single to try to move away from opera and find a new audience. She'd got together with another Sony artist, the London-based DJ and dance music star Jurgen Vries, and had sung over one key track for him in the autumn. The cover of the CD only had a sort of cartoon figure on it, and while there were several clues about Charlotte's identity and loads of people had already guessed what was going on, the whole thing was supposed to be under wraps. On the single Charlotte was being credited with just her initials, CMC (Charlotte Maria Church), a clue to anyone who thought hard about it. Then, of course there was the title: 'The Opera Song (Brave New World)'. Not exactly deep cover, but a bit of a laugh all the same.

One good thing about that track – which I thought was great, incidentally – was that it brought us together a bit more. I couldn't get hugely excited when I saw her classical albums in the shops because that sort of music didn't feel like it was anything to do with me. But we both got a buzz out of being in the Cardiff shops the first week when 'The Opera Song' was released and saw it on the shelves. Seeing someone pick it up and buy it was even cooler.

Anyway, sitting in listening to the charts on Sunday night to hear how it had done in that first week of release was like being a 12-year-old again when the charts really seemed to matter. And the news was good – Charlotte was in the Top Ten, which was an amazing result and showed that she really could reinvent herself.

Unfortunately she couldn't avoid being criticised. A posh tosser of a music critic went on to Radio 4, apparently, and said that Charlotte's voice was cracking up and she couldn't hack it any more in the opera world. Then a Welsh opera singer joined forces and agreed – and other people said Charlotte was throwing her talent away and she had never actually been that good to start with. All the papers and magazines followed it up over the next few days with big articles saying she would never be able to repeat in her 20s the success she had had in her teens. The headline HER VOICE IN JEOPARDY, CHARLOTTE'S CROAKING UP pretty much summed it all up.

For all her bravado, Charlotte always did care about what the papers said about her. She buys loads of papers and magazines and always reads as much of the coverage as possible, however hurtful it can be. While she tried to shake off this latest criticism, I could tell that it had hit her harder than most because it was professional as well as personal. She also knew this would give her even more hassle from her mum, who would see it as proof that she had been right all last year about how Charlotte was supposedly throwing everything away. The timing was also a problem. Just when she had made a big leap forward and engineered some real success by having a Top Ten dance single, everyone could only seem to focus on the negatives.

We decided to cheer ourselves up with a night in a flash hotel. There was a big charity bash going on at the Court Colman Manor hotel just up the M4 in Bridgend. We both wanted to make a splash, in different ways, so Charlotte got glammed up in a black dress that really showed off her curves, while I went for a more urban look in jeans with a cap. I reckoned we looked great together that night and we were up for a good time.

The place was beautiful and people like Jamie Shaw from the *Popstars: The Rivals* band One True Voice were good company, too. A few weeks earlier the papers had been full of stories that Charlotte and Jamie were having an affair behind my back, that they had been seen holding hands and dancing close in London clubs. It was all nonsense – and amazingly enough I had a surprising supporter when the stories were first printed. Charlotte's mother Maria, no less, defended me and my relationship with Charlotte to the press, saying there was absolutely no truth in the rumours that we were breaking up.

As it turned out, Charlotte and I were going to spend quite a bit of time with Jamie and his band-mate Matt Johnson that spring. One big night we all went to see Christina Aguilera at a gay club in London and then got turned away from having dinner at Stringfellow's because anyone who reads the papers knew that Charlotte, Jamie and Matt were all under 18.

Anyway, back at the hotel it was a good, long night, and when we finally went upstairs things got even better. Our room was amazing, all decorated in an Indian theme with a huge crimson bed in the middle of it. So we just hung out the Do Not Disturb sign and decided to hide away from the world. We ordered room service the next day, watched hours of telly, had a couple of long, hot baths and loved every minute of it.

'Charlotte looked very happy when they checked

out,' one of the receptionists told the papers the next day. For once it was true.

Next up were some great nights up in London. First of all we saw Christina Aguilera at the launch of a new mobile phone in an old meat market near the East End – proof that even the world's biggest celebrities will do almost anything if the money is right. We saw Ms Dynamite, Jerry Hall, Boy George and Jay Kay from Jamiroquai there, as well as someone who came from pretty much the same Cardiff streets as me – Shirley Bassey. Darius from *Pop Idol* was there and we talked to him for a while about the press stuff. 'Ignore it and remember that the people you love know it's all lies,' he said.

Charlotte and I were on a bit of a high that night. Her single had made it to UK No. 3, her first film was well on its way to hitting the cinemas and I had just been approached to do some professional modelling. We couldn't have been happier. Looking back I think we embarrassed ourselves a bit by spending most of the phone party just snogging in the corner.

Getting out of Wales for these big nights out seemed to take the pressure off Charlotte and me. Sure, the paparazzi were always outside the parties, the clubs and sometimes the hotels in London. But somehow they seemed to fit in at places like that. They seemed like professionals doing their job, and they always had a sense of humour when they called out to us and asked us to pose a little. They seemed to genuinely want us to look good, and they were a world away from the ones who hung around on the car bonnets outside my dad's house who wanted to snap us looking as bad as possible.

The one thing we didn't do that February was head over for Charlotte's mum's 38th birthday. Charlotte had been getting on a whole lot better with her family at this point, which was great, as the tearful, late-night phone conversations had been going on for far too long. She headed over there for Sunday lunch with them a lot, and we talked about whether I should go along as well. But neither of us had really got over the first – and last – time I had been there.

That first visit had been a month or so after Charlotte and I had started seeing each other. We had both thought it would be a relaxed 'getting to know you' meeting, and I had been on my best behaviour, determined to show I wasn't the deadbeat the papers had described. But they weren't that interested in my computer course, my ambitions to get into music production, all the things that drew Charlotte and I together. What we got instead was a lecture from her dad, the one who normally plays the good cop to her mother's very bad cop when he talks to the press.

Mr Church seemed to have a list of non-negotiable instructions for me. Where, when and how I could see Charlotte. What we could and couldn't do. What was on- and off-limits. It was like something out of a Victorian film, and when the presentation was over there didn't seem to be much room left for general conversation. Charlotte, who had left the room embarrassed when her dad had started off, came back in, realised that the atmosphere wasn't great and suggested that we leave. No more invitations had been issued, and the thought of a repeat performance over Sunday lunch didn't really appeal.

Meanwhile, Charlotte and I were both busy with meetings in the day as well. The producers of Charlotte's film were doing the final editing and working out when and where to release it. Most of the filming had been done in and around London, in areas that they thought could look like Wales, where the plot was actually set. I know Charlotte had been a bit disappointed in that, as one of her reasons for choosing the project was that it had a strong Welsh story and she had wanted to film it locally. But they said it just worked out cheaper to use London-based crews and locations, and as usual money talked. Anyway, Charlotte took me around to some of those locations and when the final result hit the screens the film-makers had certainly done some magic, because at the time we weren't convinced that they could pull it off.

About that time I was also starting to get calls asking if I was interested in doing some modelling. Nothing serious was going to go on the table until later in the year, but of course I was flattered – who wouldn't be? As part of those initial approaches I also got a call from a clothes designer asking if I wanted to wear some of his kit at a big party we had coming up. The designer had made a really sharp black/brown pinstriped suit with a matching waistcoat and cap. It was a big move from my usual style but I reckoned it would be a laugh to give it a go and in the end the suit arrived at my dad's house.

'That's the first time you've ever worn a suit, son. Should have done it years ago,' said my dad, who was convinced I would attract all the attention if I went out dressed like that.

'I've been a star since I was a child and no one's ever sent me any free clothes to wear,' was all Charlotte said as I posed around a bit. Was she joking or was she genuinely pissed off? For once I found her hard to read and couldn't tell. But I could tell that the atmosphere that night wasn't particularly good.

The big party was in London, but before we got there we had something even more exciting to do – Charlotte was going on *Top of the Pops* because 'The Opera Song' was still No.3 in the charts. They record the show in the afternoon at a studio out in west London and it's actually a pretty knackering experience. There's a lot of waiting around in dressing rooms and Charlotte also had to put in a lot of time with her choreographer to make sure she moved properly when the cameras were rolling. Her slot was recorded in two parts – some of it before the public got in the studio, some of it when the place was full. Charlotte was looking pretty foxy that day, with a cool cap hiding her hair and her performance was spot on.

Early on in the day someone said that the *Top of the Pops* editing team is so experienced with working with bad singers and useless dancers that you can be crap in real life and they'll turn things around to make you look like a star. Charlotte didn't need any help from them – and, after doing a load of interviews for the *TOTP2* show and some other publicity, we left the studio on a high.

After all that we had dinner in town and then went back to the hotel to get ready for the night's big party. It was the UKC Hero Awards event to support HIV and AIDS victims – Elton John had won the main award at it the previous year. The guest list in 2003 looked bloody impressive again and the paparazzi were out in force. Charlotte had had her hair done straight with ringlets at the end, was wearing wild red lipstick, scary high heels and a real Gothy black dress with a sort of long train over her arm.

'I paid for this myself, unlike some,' she kept saying as we got ready, and again I couldn't tell if she was joking. Earlier in the day she had also had a temporary tattoo put on her back. We both knew, when we had stood in front of the hotel mirrors half an hour earlier, that we looked great together, and the photographers agreed. Our pictures were all over the papers the next day and made it into the likes of *Hello!* and all the other celebrity magazines as well.

The ceremony itself was about as lavish as you can

get. It was at the Dorchester Hotel on Park Lane and the moment we got out of the car the camera flashes started to go off. It is a bizarre experience. You're not exactly blinded by all that, but if you're not used to it, like I wasn't, you don't really know where to look or how to act. The real party people, who go to these events all the time desperate to get their pictures in the paper, have got all this down to a fine art. They look directly towards the flashes, as if their best mate is right there, and smile like they've never been happier.

'Charlotte, over here. Come on – big smile, love.'

'Steven, round this way. Look at us.'

'Let's see your back again, Charlotte.'

'Both of you together. Over here, one more time.'

'Give her a kiss, mate.'

And so it went on while we edged, holding hands, towards the hotel door. Inside it was just as mad. There were loads of reporters, all trying to get a few lines of a quote from any famous face they could see – of which there were many. To my amazement, Charlotte and I were the ones everyone wanted to speak to the most.

'How are you two getting on?'

'Are you still in love, Charlotte?'

'Any plans for marriage we should know about?'

'Steve, is that a real tattoo on Charlotte's back?'

'How's your relationship with your mother, Charlotte?'

'Where did you get your suit from, Steven?'

It was that final one that made us laugh the most. It

wasn't often that I had out-dressed Charlotte or got any positive attention for my clothes, so it was great the next day to see that the *Mirror* called Charlotte's outfit 'stunning' but that I 'stole the show' in my pinstripes. Beat that, Posh and Becks!

Back in the big, glitzy room, everyone sat at round tables for dinner before the awards and the entertainment began. Charlotte and I were on the same table as Liza Minnelli and her soon-to-be-ex-husband David Gest. I have to say that it wasn't easy for me sitting with them, and the other people on our table. Charlotte, of course, has had years to learn how to do all the industry chit-chat and small talk. Plus, she is in the fame game and is really into all these people. Liza certainly wanted to bend Charlotte's ear about singing, their voices and changing direction mid-career. I had less to say because this wasn't really my world – and I wasn't that bothered about joining it.

Our New Year social whirl wasn't over. Charlotte needed to be massively in the public eye to promote her single, prepare people for her film and just show that she was no longer that angelic 11-year-old with the big voice that everyone thought of whenever they heard her name. Plus, to be honest, we were having a hell of a lot of fun.

Next on our list was a top fashion show, another first for me. It was London Fashion Week and we had been invited to Julien Macdonald's show at the Roundhouse in Camden, the place where everyone from Jimi

Charlotte and I would laugh together at pictures like this – how she found fame in May 1999.

When I knew her, Charlotte was desperate to get out of her mother's protective clutches.

While I liked to dress down in public, Charlotte looked great dressed up on stage.

She looked pretty innocent in this official picture for her 16th birthday.
But underneath she just wanted to live like any other teenager.

We had some great times together. *Top*: we soaked up the sun in Hawaii and *bottom*: went out together for the premiere of *I'll Be There*.

Top: Charlotte's family. From left, her grandparents, Maria, her, her dad and her aunt out together.

Bottom left: They said I was a bad influence, but I reckon we looked pretty good together.

Bottom right: *I'll Be There* might not have done that well, but Charlotte had a blast. Here she is with co-star Craig Ferguson

So in love: our faces say it all and it felt so good to be together.

Me a couple of years after we split.

Hendrix and the Rolling Stones to Pink Floyd had played. Charlotte looked brilliant that night too, with totally straight hair and a really urban look. We had both decided to dress down in jeans and leather jackets – though Charlotte kept the paparazzi happy with a sexy-as-hell black lace top that did a lot more revealing than concealing, as one of the papers said. Getting in was a real buzz, though – the place was being picketed by anti-fur protesters and their noise and all the camera flashes made the entrance feel like a war zone.

Inside it was a big night for Wales. Macdonald is Welsh and Shirley Bassey and Tom Jones were there as well. But as a teenage bloke I have to say it was the other women who I looked at the most. There were beautiful faces and bodies all around us, and as the show began almost two hours late there was plenty of time to check them all out.

Cat Deeley, the gorgeous girls from Atomic Kitten, Tara Palmer-Tomkinson, Patsy Palmer, Martine McCutcheon and Christina Aguilera were all there. Jamie Oliver was pretty much the only famous bloke we saw all evening.

What was most interesting, though, was that when the models themselves finally headed on to the catwalk they didn't do a thing for me. Too skinny, too bony, too stuck up. If you want a woman, you want a real woman, I reckon. But I shouldn't have acted quite like a kid in a sweet shop that night. Despite what the newspapers said, I was completely faithful to Charlotte – I was all flirt and no action when it came to other women – but I should have remembered that she could be insecure and sensitive about her looks. She had wowed people with her figure and her sexy lace top that night, but she still worried that I spent too long looking at other women. So when we got back to our flash hotel and got invited down to the bar for a few drinks by Christina Aguilera and her people, as far as Charlotte was concerned the answer was a big, non-negotiable 'no'.

Still, by the morning we'd patched everything up. I'd apologised for my wandering eye and I'd told Charlotte yet again that, while I might have been looking, I had no intention of touching. We were on good form for the journey back to Wales. For people who don't know our shared heritage, there's something really good about approaching and then driving over the Severn Road Bridge every time. It signals that you're nearly home. For us it also signalled that the madness of public life in London was over for a while and we were heading back to reality.

My dad, as usual, was glad to see us and have us back. He'd loved the pinstriped suit I'd worn at the Dorchester bash and had kept the cuttings of it from a whole load of newspapers and magazines. 'Bonnie and Clyde,' he said. 'You both looked like Bonnie and Clyde that night. Nobody else there looked better than you two did.' It was the kind of support all kids need, and I know that it hurt Charlotte that she didn't seem to get it from her family.

Anyway, as February got under way I had some planning to do. It was just over a year since we had first seen each other when I had been DJ'ing at that party. Charlotte's 17th birthday was approaching, which we had decided was the official anniversary of us properly dating. I wanted to do something special, but I didn't realise I had competition.

Charlotte's mate Naomi told me that Maria was talking about organising a grand party with hundreds of guests. I kind of felt that Charlotte wouldn't really be up for that, especially as I had a feeling that my invitation might mysteriously get lost in the post. But I also knew that I had to play it safe, put up my idea for the night and then leave the final decision with Charlotte.

Fortunately, when the time came she wanted what I wanted – a quiet, romantic night at our favourite Chinese restaurant with just Naomi, Joshua, Charlotte and me. I'd spoken to the managers beforehand to make sure everything went perfectly on the night. We had our favourite table, great service and I'd sorted the money out the day before so we didn't even get presented with a bill. I also arranged for some white flowers to be delivered to the table at the end of the meal – lilies, Charlotte's favourite. It was the first time I had ever bought a girl flowers and with Charlotte it finally felt right to do so.

After all our big, high-profile nights out in London it was great to just get back to normal at home with our closest friends. Charlotte and I both seemed to spend most of that night out smiling at each other and at the world in general. This felt like real life again, and it felt good. What also felt good was the fact that Charlotte was angling for a raise and I was about to start earning some serious money myself.

When we first met, Charlotte was only getting about £50 a week in cash to spend. True, she also had Jeff and Mark waiting in the wings most of the time to take her anywhere she wanted to go, so it wasn't like she needed bus fares or cash for a minicab. Any other big expenses that could be related to her career could also be justified with her accountant and paid for out of her trust fund. But, in terms of cash to spend in the shops on day-to-day stuff, she had just the £50. After pointing out that this effectively left her far poorer than me, and almost all of her former school friends, Charlotte persuaded Sony to raise the money to the dizzy heights of £150 a week – something that apparently drove Maria mad.

Around this time Charlotte also started to try and bring the ridiculous claims about the size of her trust fund back down to earth. Over the past year she had laughed with me at the figures in the so-called 'Rich Lists' that claimed she was worth a minimum of £16 million – far more than the likes of Kate Moss, Rio Ferdinand, Jude Law and Craig David. The reality,

Charlotte knew, was good, but not that good. Apparently £6 million was a more likely figure, though this was not the only surprise Charlotte was to get when she sat down with her money people and lawyers that spring. For years it had been drummed into her that she would have to wait until she was 21 to get free access to the cash. In fact she could take control three years sooner, at 18. Despite that, back in February 2003, both of us were more concerned with making money than spending it.

I'd had my picture in the papers quite a lot, and, while most of the time the newspapers seemed to pick shots that made me look as bad and as rough as possible to illustrate their belief that I was a troublemaker, some people had seen beyond that. That was why I had been asked to wear the special pinstriped suit out in public. And when I did, other people must have started to take notice as well. It turned out there was a chance I could be in demand as a model.

A lot of the initial introductions and discussions came through Intech, the people who were already helping me with my music production. They called me up and sent stuff to me to look at. Charlotte and I read the messages half-thinking it must be a joke or a wind-up. Apparently people thought I had the sort of edgy, urban look that was in style and some agencies wanted to have some meetings to discuss it all. Not really convinced anything would come of it, I agreed to do some test shots.

I had actually done a very small bit of modelling long before I met Charlotte. One old friend of a friend, Tamzin Proctor – of whom more later – had roped me into a catwalk show at the Marriott Hotel, where I had done my stuff wearing a selection of clothes from the likes of M&S, Wardrobe and House of Fraser in front of around two hundred people. The reaction from the audience had been pretty good, and I had loved the atmosphere behind the scenes as well. A lot of people are involved in fashion shows, and there's a real buzz about them. I got a taste for that world back then, though I hadn't done much to follow it up until the Intech people gave me a push a couple of years later.

Charlotte was busy with meetings of her own, so off I went to London to meet four big agencies, including Storm, Models 1 and Select. It's pretty much an ordeal from the start. You're being judged from the minute you walk through their doors – or even before, as I was convinced they might be looking out of the windows to see visitors off their guard as well. The staff on the receptions were exactly what you would imagine – gorgeous – but they were a lot nicer and friendlier than I had expected. So I sat my way through a load of Polaroid shoots and listened to them talk about all their connections with magazines, fashion designers, advertisers and film companies.

I also got to talk to some of the other models, male and female, who were waiting for appointments or castings as well. You don't make any new friends in those kind of quick chats, and with the men you get a sense of a competition. But I didn't dislike anyone I spoke to and felt this could be a world I would enjoy being part of. What I thought would help get the newspapers off my back as well was the fact that I was there on my own. Charlotte was over 150 miles away in Cardiff and I was being judged totally on how I looked and acted. Anything I did achieve would be on my merits alone, and that felt pretty good – especially as all the early feedback was positive.

After speaking to all the different agency people I finally decided to sign up with Select. They were the friendliest and I liked their style. They had good links with major names like Hugo Boss, Moschino, *Vogue* and *Cosmopolitan*. They had had the likes of Rachel Hunter, Helena Christensen, Sienna Miller and Stella Tennant on their books and the model sheet they gave me to take away said they represented 'the UK's brightest, biggest and most successful male and female modelling talents'. I decided I wanted a bit of that to rub off on me and I willed the train home to go faster so I could tell Charlotte about my big day.

Over the next couple of days I was really excited about the way the modelling meetings had gone, and for once I was pleased about the way the press was treating it. 'The shots Steve did for us looked amazing. He's got a really great look, sexy and urban. He will be a massive hit, like a young Nick Kamen from the Levi's advert,' Select's spokeswoman told one reporter, which was more than I could have ever hoped for. Other reports followed suit and I was finally given some positive vibes. One paper even dredged up the old 'Angel's Delight' heading to put over one of the new photos of me. I really thought I might have turned a corner, that all the 'teenage tearaway' stuff was going to be forgotten and I'd get treated like anyone else trying to make a go of things.

As if all that wasn't good enough, I also got asked to a big promotional shoot in Majorca to help build up a proper portfolio of pictures. There were about 15 people there in total, including the models, agency staff, photographers and stylists and the whole experience was bizarre and amazing. In some ways it was like being back in Ibiza. But this time I reckoned I could be about to earn some serious money rather than just working in bars and doing some DJ jobs. This was the start of a proper, professional career and I was serious as hell about it.

After the Majorca shots there were a lot of castings and meetings to go to – jobs for the likes of Harvey Nichols, H&M, *Wallpaper** and so on. We did shoots in hotels, flash London apartments and mansions in the country. Like I said, sometimes you're not really with people long enough to make friends and there is a lot of competition between all the guys. But I did have some good laughs with the likes of fellow Welshman Steve Jones, who got some great Versace contracts and is now making it as a big-time presenter on Channel

Four. A year later I read in the papers that he even got flown to LA by Halle Berry – she had liked him so much when he had interviewed her that she wanted to have dinner with him in her favourite restaurant. Way to go, Steve!

In April 2003, Charlotte and I were off to America on our own steam. First of all, Charlotte had been invited to Hawaii by IBM to perform at some huge motivational and training event for its staff. It was a one-off gig with a big pay cheque – money which, as ever, would go straight into Charlotte's trust fund. Then a lot of other events were tied on to the original invitation. There were film meetings in LA, plus meetings there with Sony, her record company. Then there was that really big, one-night-only concert at the Aladdin Hotel in Las Vegas.

'Come with me, Steve.'

We were on our way back from the cinema one night when Charlotte started talking about the trip and how much work it would involve. The IBM concert was an unusual one because there wouldn't be ticket sales to worry about, but Charlotte knew she still had to put on a great show so she was nervous about it. And knowing that the big Vegas show was hanging over everything would make the whole trip more tense for her.

'We could combine it with a holiday in Hawaii. It would be the first time we've had a holiday together, Steve. Come on, we deserve that after everything we've had to put up with over the past year.'

After more than a year of saying no every time Charlotte asked me to go away with her, I finally heard myself say yes. A holiday in the sun would be fantastic. And yes, we did deserve a break. Going to Hawaii would give us a few days of freedom from the photographers and the reporters. I wanted to swim in an outdoor pool with my girlfriend and have dinner with her by the sea. I wanted to walk barefoot along a beach with her in the moonlight and maybe catch a sunrise over the ocean. It was going to be fantastic.

CHAPTER ELEVEN

MY BARBIE IS A CRACK WHORE

The first thing Charlotte and I learned when we decided to go on the trip together was that it was a hell of a long way to Hawaii. The next thing we learned was that big business-class seats are so far apart from each other that it's not easy to snuggle up and have some fun under the blankets with the one you love. Charlotte and I didn't exactly get to join the Mile High Club, but we gave it a pretty good try all the same.

Travelling with Charlotte was different to spending time with her at home. On any normal day in London or Cardiff it was amazing how often we could go places totally unnoticed. If people aren't expecting to see a famous face they often won't recognise any that do walk through their doors. But airports are where people tend to be on the lookout for stars, so we got stared at and stopped a lot as we checked in and headed through passport control to the private lounge. Charlotte, as usual, treated everyone well and got a lot of good wishes from people. Several actually said that they thought the press were being really unfair to her and that she should just live her life the way she wanted to. We were holding hands at that point and I knew she meant it when she said that was exactly what she intended to do.

Flying business class to America was also very different to flying economy to Europe, which was what I'd been doing last time I was on a plane. As it was a work trip for Charlotte, we had several of her management and PR people coming out with us, but we had all met several times before and everyone got on well and was looking forward to the trip. What we didn't have on board was Charlotte's mother or father, which certainly suited me.

'Ladies and gentlemen, fasten your seatbelts, please.'

I love takeoff. The sudden speed, the noise, the feeling that nothing can stop you now and you are on your way somewhere great. Charlotte, however, hates it, just like she pretty much hates flying in general, so we held hands as our plane left the runway and started to climb.

Not even the glass of champagne you can get if you are flying at the front of the plane calmed Charlotte down, though the stewardesses and stewards were so nice to us that after a while she began to relax. There was a bar in the cabin where you can sit, have a drink and a chat, so we took up position there for a while so Charlotte could take her mind off the fact that we were 35,000 feet above the Atlantic Ocean.

About ten hours later we landed in LA for a quick change of plane before getting a second flight out over the Pacific to Hawaii. It was early evening when we finally landed in Honolulu. And it was hot. The airport itself is practically perfect – you don't just feel like you've arrived on a romantic desert island, you feel like you've stepped back in time. It's tropical with palm trees everywhere and local people in grass skirts really do come out to put garlands round your necks. We walked across the tarmac to a terminal building that looks like something from the 1950s. Throw in the band playing island music and the warm holiday air, and you've come about as far from Cardiff as you can.

'We are going to have so much fun,' I whispered to Charlotte as we got on our final flight to one of Hawaii's other islands, where we were staying. Everything outside the plane windows now was dark, black and exciting.

Our hotel, when we finally got there, was everything we wanted it to be and well worth the long, long journey from Britain. It was called the Fairmont Orchid Resort on the Kohala coast of one of the biggest islands in the group. And it was huge – acres and acres of grounds with pools, beaches and palm trees everywhere. Charlotte and I had a stunning two-bed apartment, stuffed with fresh flowers and right on the ocean – we could lie in bed and hear the sounds of the waves. The hotel laid on anything we wanted so we just wandered the beaches looking for turtles, swam and snorkelled a bit in the sea, floated around in one of the pools, and just relaxed among the palm trees.

We also tried to pay our dues in small talk and chit-chat. Our first five days on the island were supposed to be pure holiday for the two of us, but as usual work got in the way pretty soon. For our first jet-lag-free evening the business people and Charlotte's management had arranged what they call a 'meet and greet' dinner for us. That was the cue for Charlotte to turn on the star power and chat away with the executives. She was good at it – she's had years of experience – but I still struggled and pretty much hated every minute. I just couldn't find much common ground with the business people all around us.

The next day there was much worse, however. We were both happily loafing around by the pool, trying to forget about the rest of the world when Charlotte's mobile rang. It was her mother. And as usual she was shouting. Apparently we had created a massive media storm the moment we had arrived in LA. There had been a couple of photographers there, as there always were wherever we were, and they had taken some pictures of us getting off the plane and through the airport. Just how bad did we look in those pictures, I was thinking, as Charlotte shrugged her shoulders and looked questioningly at me as her mother built up steam.

Then it came out. It had been Charlotte's T-shirt, the one she had pulled on for the remaining part of the flight when we had our stopover in Los Angeles. The one that said 'My Barbie is a Crack Whore' across the front of it.

I have to say I liked that T-shirt. I thought it was funny and that Charlotte looked good in it. She always looked good in tight tops like that, and it wasn't as if she had bought it in some dodgy sex shop or had it made especially for her. We found out later that it was actually one of the best-selling British high-street designs of the year, so Charlotte was hardly on her own in buying and wearing it.

Unfortunately she was on her own in being splashed all over the newspapers with it on. Her mum, protective as ever, had gone ballistic when she had seen it.

'What were you thinking of?' I could hear her yelling down the phone when I got closer to Charlotte to try and find out what was going on. 'Didn't you realise you were going to be photographed? Didn't you think about what people would say? "My Barbie is a crack whore"! My God, Charlotte, have you gone completely mad?' And so it went on.

'Mum. Look, I'm sorry,' Charlotte tried to interrupt as some of the other hotel guests around the pool started to look up. Everyone could tell from Charlotte's face and body language that something bad had happened.

'I didn't realise that there would be photographers. I never even thought about the T-shirt.' She held the phone away from her ear as her mother started shouting again. 'Look, Mum. Everything else was packed and it was comfortable, OK?'

Then I heard Charlotte's dad take over the conversation. 'Sorry, Dad,' Charlotte said to him, sitting fully upright now with tears suddenly forming in her eyes. I reached over to hold her free hand as she tied to blink them away. 'Look, I'll go and bury it in the sand now, if that'll help. I promise I'll never wear it again.'

'What the hell was all that about?'

'They've put pictures in the papers at home of me in the Barbie T-shirt. They were taken when we got off the plane in LA. And the reporters are all back saying I'm going off the rails again.'

We sat in paradise, in silence for quite a long time, both thinking about what had happened, both furious that our holiday could be ruined by something so trivial.

'Let's go for a swim.'

After a while we smiled at each other, knowing there was nothing we could do about the mess now. We tried to ignore the glances from the other guests and slipped into the pool. The water was warm and the sun was strong. Once again the world was causing us trouble, but as we lay back in the shallow end of our pool looking up at the sky we also knew that as long as we stuck together we could get through it. I kissed her on the lips and whispered that I loved her.

'Steve, can we have a word with you?'

Some of Charlotte's American PR people came over

later in the week while I was having a snooze under the palm trees. At first, as usual, I feared the worst. If the PRs were coming up to me when I was on my own it must mean something even more awful than before had been written in the papers, this time maybe in the American press, which tended to be far kinder to Charlotte than the UK papers.

I tried to think what it could possibly be. With the Barbie T-shirt out of the way the two of us had just had a nice, romantic few days. Charlotte had been rehearsing for her gig, and the men in suits seemed happy with the way things were going. My heart just sank to think what could possibly have gone wrong now.

But the PR people didn't have any bad news. On the contrary, they had a business proposition for me. 'We've got some casting going on in LA next week and we'd like you to take part in them. And if you do, we've got some other people over from New York we'd like to meet with you, as well.'

I could hardly believe it, especially when they told me a bit about some of the people they were dealing with. Producers and agents who had worked on films like *Pulp Fiction* and the *Mission Impossible* films were among the names mentioned. As usual I did think this might be a wind-up – I don't think I'll ever really get over that first conversation with the *News of the World* – but the PR people were clearly serious, the way a lot of Americans are. After taking the first few steps to do some modelling in Britain, it looked as if I might take a big leap in America. I was scared, but over the moon.

Charlotte seemed happy for me when I caught up with her in our room later on. But I have to admit I could have done with just a bit more enthusiasm. Her biggest worry seemed to be that we might not have time for my meetings while we were in LA because her schedule there was already quite tight. I nodded, strangely disappointed, and flicked on the big-screen TV. If an opportunity like this was being put in front of me, then I could hardly let it slip through my fingers. I had to make sure I had time for those meetings. I'd have moved them both to make sure Charlotte could see the people she needed to see if the tables had been reversed.

The first real warning bell I had felt in the whole 14 months we had spent together went off somewhere deep inside me that evening in Hawaii. It wasn't something I really thought about at the time, and when I did I tried to tell myself I was making a mistake, making something out of nothing. Charlotte was my girlfriend, so of course she was on my side. Of course she wanted me to succeed. I pushed every other thought aside and focused on that. It was the first of many mistakes I would make that year.

CHAPTER TWELVE
A WEEK IN LA

They say that you either love or hate Los Angeles. I have to say I don't really understand it. It's hard to work out exactly where the heart of it is and where you are. The individual areas are cool enough – Malibu, Santa Barbara, the Hollywood Hills and so on – and all the freeways are pretty amazing just in themselves. But Charlotte and I never quite felt that we got the real pulse of the place.

We flew in from Hawaii after the day after Charlotte's big concert. She had sung a pretty long set of her old classical and opera stuff – no room for her dance tracks or new image there. The IBM crowd certainly seemed to like it and they treated Charlotte like a queen both before and after it. I liked that because she deserved it.

The other big cliché about LA is that everyone spends half their life in their cars – and that's certainly where I spent a hell of a lot of my time in the city.

Charlotte's meetings seemed to take priority over mine, and a lot of the time I was left sitting in her car while she headed into the various offices and agencies. There were worse cars to be in, as it was huge, air-conditioned and had blacked-out windows so I could stare at people without them knowing I was there. But that gets boring after an hour or so – especially in LA, where not that many people seemed to be walking in the first place.

Charlotte and I were staying in a massive mansion in Bel Air that was owned by someone in her management company. It was like something on a film set, with a huge pool surrounded by palm trees, a cinema, maids' quarters and parking for what seemed like millions of cars, including jeeps and vast four-wheel-drive things that looked like early Hummers. We hung out a bit in Melrose, home of the likes of Justin Timberlake and Britney Spears, where there are loads of cool little shops that Charlotte loved. Her manager's daughter was on hand to show us a good time and we headed out clubbing a few nights with her – getting the full VIP treatment all the way.

Curled up in bed together afterwards, Charlotte and I thought that the whole thing on nights out was like an episode of *Beverly Hills 90210*. Everywhere we went we were with the young, rich kids of the city's movers and shakers. Everyone seemed to have way too much money and confidence. They all looked like models, but no one looked real. The music, though, was exactly what we liked. We hung out in some pure R&B clubs and then had a surreal experience when someone we had met took us back to her offices at 2am. We nodded at the surprised security guards as she led us towards the lifts, then found out why we were there. The view of the city from the top of her glass tower was amazing. Charlotte and I held hands watching the lights twinkle through the smog. We felt like king and queen of the world.

The fact that Charlotte was so busy meant that I didn't get to see as many modelling or acting people in LA as I had hoped to. The ones I did see – especially the guy from New York – were great, though, and wanted me send over as many professional pictures as possible, as soon as possible. Charlotte's management back in Britain had most of the good shots, so I got in touch, asked them to help out and kept my fingers crossed. This really could be the start of something big, I thought.

When Charlotte and I had dinner that night before leaving for Las Vegas – where she was performing and I had more meetings being planned – I don't think I had ever been happier or more excited about the future. If only I had known that things weren't going to work out quite the way I had hoped.

CHAPTER THIRTEEN
THE FILM BUSINESS

Some big changes were being planned in Cardiff when we got back from Las Vegas. The biggest was the news that Charlotte's mum and dad seemed to have finally worked out that their baby had grown up and wanted her own life. I think they realised that this meant they, too, would need new lives of their own. So the big house in Coryton was put on the market for some £650,000 and they announced to the press that they were easing out of show business altogether. They wanted to run a small hotel instead.

It was a time when relations between our two families could have really thawed – and to a small degree they did. I wasn't exactly an honoured guest at the new hotel when it was up and running, and Charlotte and I weren't offered the use of any bridal suite there. But at least when Maria spoke to the newspapers she didn't seem to be so full of anger about me – she seemed able to accept that Charlotte and I made each other happy. We felt we were finally moving forwards.

Meanwhile Charlotte's new mix-and-match career was still raising eyebrows – she had been invited to speak to the Oxford Union at Oxford University. Pretty scary stuff for a girl from South Wales who had left school at 16, we thought, trying to work out just how tough the audience was likely to be. Then someone told us that past speakers hadn't just included the likes of Bill Clinton and Nelson Mandela – Kermit the Frog had also done the honours one year, apparently. Suddenly the prospect didn't seem so daunting, though in the event Charlotte wouldn't have time to accept the challenge straightaway.

What Charlotte was spending all her time doing was getting ready for the release of her first film. Nobody knew how well it would do at the box office, but the key thing, we were told, was to get Charlotte's name and face out there as much as possible to give it as much publicity as possible. That meant heading back and forwards to London, with Charlotte giving interviews and posing for photographs at the drop of a hat. Without realising it I had morphed into the role of silent supporter, there to hold the bags, watch the clock and give whatever support I could. It wasn't exactly my dream role, but Charlotte was my girlfriend and I had to hope that one day she might do the same for me.

Charlotte's publicity blitz and the photos that were taken as part of it had an immediate impact. The most eye-catching were the shots she did for the June issue of *The Face*. They put her on the cover with the dream headline: CHARLOTTE CHURCH: THE BIRTH OF A BRITISH SUPERSTAR. The main picture of Charlotte was so different to her normal look that it was almost hard to recognise her. She was called 'the vamp' and I thought she looked a bit like Miss Whiplash. Apart from huge red lips, they had put masses of make-up on her, so her face was totally powdered-out and white. She had a hat with a veil on her head, tied-up straight hair and just enough cleavage to tease. It was sexy as hell and a million miles from any Charlotte Church pictures anyone had seen before. It must have been hard for people to believe she was still just 17.

Inside the magazine the pictures were even more amazing. Again, they had glammed her up to the nines, with some sort of 1950s retro hats and gloves that made her look like an old-fashioned movie star. In the interview she was called 'Britain's Britney' and talked about everything from drugs, her weight, her mother – and me.

On drugs she said exactly what I knew she thought – that she had been offered drugs loads of times (the first time, she had told me, had been when she was just 14 in New York) but had always said no. 'Stuff like E, I'd be too scared I'd get a dodgy one and I'd die. And I don't want to die,' she told the magazine.

What she said about her body made me laugh. 'Yeah, my arse is a bit big but I'm happy with myself,' she said, adding that her management and agents were constantly telling her she needed to lose weight if she wanted to get film, television or advertising work. Those kind of instructions are hard to hear, and I know they upset Charlotte sometimes, so it was good to see her so grounded on the subject. I couldn't count the number of times I had grabbed her arse and told her how good she looked: hopefully that might have contributed to the confidence she now had about her body.

Charlotte was honest about her mother, admitting that career-wise they had moved apart but that they still spoke all the time. When it came to the really personal stuff I still don't know quite how I feel about things. I was later accused of doing a 'kiss and tell' on Charlotte, even though I never said one word about sex. But here, out of nowhere, Charlotte herself was going into a hell of a lot of detail about the night she first slept with me, even how she and her friend Naomi had aimed to lose their virginity at the same time.

'Naomi and I had talked about contraception and we were well protected. It was never a competition to lose our virginity, there was no peer pressure. None of my friends are like that. If one of us doesn't want to do something then that's it, we leave it alone. I did it when it felt it was right.' But I had known nothing of her plans, Charlotte told the reporter. 'He didn't know that I had decided to do it that night. It was a surprise for him. But it was important that I knew I loved Steven before I slept with him.'

I have to say it is a funny feeling having the world told about your sex life. But I knew just how much Charlotte wanted to prove to the world that she was a grown-up woman, and I knew how much pressure her people were putting on her to promote her film. So I had to just accept all that as part of the package of being in love with her.

Other people were also getting burned that summer. The day before Father's Day the *News of the World* ran a page claiming that Charlotte had accused her real dad of being a gold-digger and that he had never been in touch until she was rich and famous. I never found out if Charlotte had really spoken to the paper about all that, even though it was quoting her directly. But these were depressing, very personal days.

Fortunately the long-awaited release of *I'll Be There* meant that there were some fun, if stressful, days coming up as well. Most of the stress, as usual, came from the fact that Charlotte's parents and I were still far from best friends and the press had realised that the film premiere was one occasion where we might have to meet in public. As if that weren't bad enough, we might have to do it twice – because the film was being launched both in Cardiff and London.

Charlotte had been determined to have a big bash for the film in her home town. It was a Welsh film, she was proudly Welsh, and so far she has still not left Cardiff to live in London, America or anywhere else. So she thought Wales deserved a share of the action and I prayed it would repay the favour by supporting her on her big night. Unfortunately, before that night we had to sort out the guest list – which meant working out how her mum and I would get along.

'Steve, I need one of you there. I can't stand in front of all the photographers on my own. The papers will say I've been dumped by both my mum and my boyfriend.'

'Well, we need to find out what your mum wants to do. I just don't want this to kick off World War Three.'

As it turned out, Charlotte's mum famously said she would rather stay at home to watch *EastEnders* with a cup of tea than go to the Welsh premiere, so that suited us all. The premiere itself was taking place in the flash new UCI cinema not far from my dad's home – the cinema where Charlotte and I had seen our first film together more than a year earlier and where we went back all the time. But on 9 June 2003 the place looked like downtown Hollywood. The police had put up crash barriers for the crowds, a huge bank of photographers were pushing behind a rope by the entrance and there was even a red carpet on the floor. Both of us had to laugh at how different it all was.

Before heading out that night there had been all the usual worries over what we would wear. As the night had been set aside as a relaxed premiere for Charlotte's friends, she had decided to dress down and wore tight jeans and a cropped, sleeveless top. Despite this I kind of felt that it was still a big event, and didn't want Charlotte's mum saying I had let her daughter down by dressing badly on such a big night. So I smartened up in an all-white outfit of a big shirt and trousers.

'So, we're gorgeous, don't you think?'

We were both in the big bathroom at my dad's home looking at ourselves in the mirror and I wanted to check Charlotte was happy.

'We're looking good,' she said, smiling. 'Let me practise my speech one more time.' Charlotte was due to say a few words at the cinema alongside the director and co-star Craig Ferguson, and that was adding to the stress of the evening. But her speech was good and we were ready to go.

The place was packed and Charlotte had lots of autographs to sign and people to speak to before we even got through the doors. Once inside we got rushed away and taken to our seats where two of my sisters, two of my aunts, Naomi, Becky and Joshua were all waiting for us. At premieres you don't get all the usual adverts and 'coming shortly' previews, so there was a real sense of excitement in the air as the lights finally went down. As they did, I realised just how nervous Charlotte was – and how nervous I was for her.

'You're going to be great,' I whispered. 'They'll love you. Trust me.'

But seeing yourself on screen, so huge, is a terrifying thing and Charlotte cringed and sank down in her seat as soon as her face appeared in front of us. She said later that she felt like she was putting herself up to be judged and that she was terrified about knowing what everyone's verdict is straightaway, because she knew they would all be talking about it in the lobby as soon as the lights went up. Fortunately for Charlotte, she was in the centre of her gang of biggest friends and everyone else in the cinema seemed to be on her side as well.

At first I almost had a panic attack, though. Where's Charlotte's name? Who are all these people? I kept thinking as the opening credits rolled. Name after name was going up there, but no Charlotte. But then, suddenly, there it was. 'And introducing Charlotte Church.' All on its own, big letters filling the screen. She really was a star.

What was brilliant about the film was how professional it was. Because you know people who are in something, you somehow imagine it won't be as slick as Hollywood. But this one was. Charlotte's voice starts it right off – she is singing in an empty church. She is playing a girl with an amazing singing voice who lives with her mum and dreams of a good relationship with her real dad. It was pretty much a role Charlotte was born to play, and gave her the chance to sing a load of new and old songs.

'I look fat in this next bit. I look like a whale,' Charlotte whispered to me in one scene towards the end of the movie. But of course she didn't. I think Charlotte still has mixed feelings about the film, probably because it was her first as an actress. But I thought it was brilliant and, thank God, when the closing credits started to roll in Cardiff there was a massive round of applause. People genuinely seemed to have loved it. I saw tears in Charlotte's eyes as we held hands, relieved it was all over and fantastically proud of what we had seen. There were even cheers as we finally got up from our seats and headed out into the lobby.

After the screening Warner Brothers had arranged a private party for a couple of dozen of us at the St David's Hotel on Cardiff Bay. Going back to that huge hotel always brings back memories for me – not all of them good. The bad memory is of the *News of the World* sting when I walked into their trap. But the good memory outweighs the bad, and that is of the time before Charlotte and I had officially started dating, when I ran over to see her between planning meetings about the film we had just seen. Right now that seemed so long ago.

I will always remember that fresh, happy Charlotte who tried to get away from her minders to speak to me. The nervous 15-year-old who kissed me and who promised so much. Everything seemed so simple back then. We were just two teenagers who liked each other, fancied each other and wanted to go out with each other. We had no idea how many obstacles would be in our way or how hard we would have to fight to stay together.

Of course in June 2003, on the night of the after-show party, we didn't have any complaints about our situation. We were both on a huge high, both wanting to stay close and drink in the atmosphere. We had survived all the things life had thrown at us, and here we still were – together in a room with all our joint friends and some of my family. No wonder all the photographs of that night show us grinning like a pair of idiots.

The party itself was brilliant. There was a big sit-down meal for everyone, followed by drinks, some decent music and plenty of chilling out. The Americans and the London-based executives from Warner Brothers were really cool and everyone got on brilliantly. By 2am we were knackered, though, and decided our part of the party was over. We headed upstairs to the top floor, where we had a penthouse suite – just reward for that night's star of the show. I remember collapsing on the huge bed and kicking off my shoes as Charlotte flopped beside me. We just grinned at each other.

'Brilliant night,' was all I could find the energy to say.

'Thanks for being here,' Charlotte replied, reaching out for my hand. 'I just wish I hadn't looked so bloody fat on the screen.'

'You looked fantastic. The whole film was brilliant. You've made it.'

Then we got a bit romantic and I'm too embarrassed to repeat any of it. What we did do when all the gooey conversation was over was sleep. Right through into the middle of the next morning, when my dad, a couple of my sisters and my mum came round to find out how the party had ended. It was about 4pm when we finally checked out and headed home. All the hotel staff said nice things as we passed, congratulating Charlotte on her leap into films. Altogether it had been a brilliant 24 hours.

Next up was the London premiere in Leicester Square, where Charlotte's parents and the rest of her family were planning to be centre stage. After the dressed-down, casual look at the Cardiff show Charlotte was determined to pull out all the stops in London. She wanted to go for a bit of old-fashioned film-star glamour, and had been loaned a bunch of diamonds worth almost as much as the house her parents had just sold, or so she told me. Walking up the red carpet in London was a lot harder than in Cardiff, she said later, because there were so many more reporters and television crews all wanting a quote, a smile or a soundbite. The hot topic for most of the questions was the fact that I wasn't there, but that her mum was.

'Mum doesn't like Steven at all but there's nothing I can do about it,' she said, trying to make light of it all by answering one of the questions with a laugh. 'I'm sure there are thousands of mums who don't like their daughter's boyfriends so it's normal. But I get on well with my mum and I have a fantastic time with Steven, so I get the best of both worlds.'

Then, as the flashbulbs went crazy, Charlotte disappeared into the Leicester Square cinema to watch and listen to herself one more time. I was actually more nervous about Charlotte for this performance than I had been for the one in Cardiff. The London-based critics were the ones that really mattered. They were the ones writing the reviews that could make or break the film, and once the lights went down in Leicester Square there was nothing anyone could do if they hated it.

The film's director Craig Ferguson had already said that there was 'no question' that Charlotte was a good actress who had won her part in the film on her merits. But Charlotte, as usual, was still preparing for the worst. 'I'll probably get slagged off but I'll take it on the chin,' she said on the red carpet. 'At first I was thinking: "I can't do this, I can't act," but it did get better and better' she said when one of the reporters asked her how it had felt after her first day's filming.

Straight after the screening Charlotte and her family headed to Soho House for a celebratory dinner, and it was from the ladies' loo there that I got a text saying that she would be with me soon. She headed back to their hotel, got changed out of her posh premiere dress into a sexy black skirt and a cool oriental top and joined me and the gang at the So:Ho nightclub on Shaftesbury Avenue. Obviously Charlotte was still under 18, so theoretically unable to drink, and probably wasn't even supposed to be there. But she was sophisticated enough to pull it off and we had a lot of fun. It was like some of the nights the previous autumn when we had done our own thing but made sure we ended up in the same place. There was something secretive about it and it made us feel like we were defying all the odds just to be together.

'I'm a film star,' Charlotte joked the next morning at the crack of dawn as she headed out to do a breakfast television show. 'It's real. It's actually happened. I can't believe it.' Later on in the day we headed over to see her name in lights outside the Leicester Square cinema. It was real and it had actually happened. Charlotte had climbed a new mountain.

Unfortunately the good feelings didn't last, because pretty soon the reviews came in. They made us feel like we were banging our heads against a brick wall. A lot of them seemed to have been written before the critics had even seen the film – they were just designed to show off some new jokes they had thought of at Charlotte's expense. Channel Four gave the film just 1 out of 10 and said: 'Judging from her wooden and expressionless performance, a real church would have been more animated.'

What I don't think the reviewers realise is that jokey little comments like that can have a huge effect on people. If viewers stay away because of them it's not just Charlotte who gets hurt; it's all the other people who worked really hard on the film and had high hopes for it. Sadly, viewers did stay away, which the papers were also thrilled to be able to report. The UCG in Cardiff, where we had been for the premiere, said it took just £600 for *I'll Be There* against £12,000 for *2 Fast 2 Furious* in the same week. Down the road in Newport they said they took even less, with just 108 people paying to see it. In the film's second week of release the figures across the country were even worse, apparently, and it soon disappeared from trace.

Charlotte, thankfully, had expected the criticism and was fine with the way things had worked out. 'I wanted to see what it was like making a film, it was brilliant fun and I don't regret it for a minute,' she said when people asked her. 'I'm proud of the film and I think it could have done better, but you can't expect to win at everything first time.'

Fortunately Charlotte and I could easily put all this behind us, because we had something else to occupy our minds that summer, apart from bitter critics. We had a home to kit out. We had finally decided to get our own place.

CHAPTER FOURTEEN

A PENTHOUSE
AND A PUPPY

Living in my dad's house for nearly a year had been fun. But the place wasn't really big enough for three and after the smoking incident the atmosphere there had got almost as tense as it would have been if we had been living with her mum and dad in the new Church Hotel on Cathedral Road. We wanted our own place, but not the house her management had sorted out in Pontcanna, which had never really felt like a home. Cardiff, back then, was booming and flash new apartment blocks were springing up all over it. City centre living was cool again, so Charlotte and I decided to join the party.

The place we decided on was stunning. It was pretty much brand new and was right on the bay next to the St David's Hotel. There were new bars and cafes all around and the whole area was buzzing. We had two big bedrooms, two bathrooms, all the walls were white and clean, and floor-to-ceiling glass windows opened from the living room on to a huge balcony looking out over the water. Our views on the other side were towards the new development of the bay with all the new shops and restaurants. It couldn't have been better.

'Should I carry you over the threshold?' I joked the day we moved in.

'The wedding rumours weren't true, remember?' was all I got in reply, so I didn't. Once inside we just ran around the rooms like two crazy children, thrilled about all this space, privacy and freedom. It didn't feel like a fresh start, because we didn't need one. But it did feel like a new adventure. It felt like we were growing up.

Masses of our friends came round those first few days, bringing plants, little presents and bottles of champagne. Charlotte and I had a new wave of domesticity – she did all the cleaning, we both did big shops in Asda and tried to cook some good meals in our shiny new kitchen. We had said long ago that neither of us wanted to think about getting married until we were in our mid-20s. But as we lay in bed with our own front door firmly locked against the rest of the world, it felt strangely as if we had.

The apartment building had a gym in it so we decided to go on a keep fit campaign. The idea was to go every morning and really work on our bodies and our fitness. We had great plans and the first time we went down there we had a real laugh. Unfortunately we laughed more than we actually exercised. Charlotte reckoned her asthma meant she couldn't really do as much on the running machines or bikes as she wanted. In the end we probably spent more time there just chatting and flicking through magazines than working out. But they were good times.

Now we were in our own home, Charlotte decided it was time to buy a dog. We got a cute little puppy called Sasha, who went everywhere with her. Charlotte also got two little lizards that were slightly less cute, especially when you had to feed them live crickets and maggots.

One thing we hadn't noticed when we had picked the flat was the fact that it wasn't always quite as private as we had hoped. We had porters downstairs on the main door, which was important for security reasons. But, while Charlotte's fans couldn't get into our new home, it turned out that they could see in. We were right on the route of one of the open-topped tourist buses that took people around the city, and listening to their live commentaries told us that our balcony and living room windows had become as much an attraction as the castle and the Millennium Stadium. Dozens of tourists, all with cameras, could be on a bus or a boat outside the flat at a time, all desperate to get a glimpse of us. The first time they did – before we realised what was going on – we had been having a bit of a kiss and a cuddle in the sunshine. After that we tried to behave as soon as we saw one of the green-and-yellow buses trundle towards us.

If one of the buses had gone by on the night of one of our flat-warming parties, the tourists might have got an even better photograph, though. I've no idea what triggered it, but one night, when a whole gang of our mates were over, Charlotte took her top off and ran round the flat in her bra, refusing to get fully dressed again for ages.

Like many other young couples, our other big challenge that summer was furnishing our new home. For all the rumours of Charlotte's multi-million-pound trust fund, the fact was that neither of us had a huge amount of cash, so we had to prioritise and take things slow. Charlotte's taste is pretty modern – she liked clean, simple furniture and we both liked the idea of having big leather sofas to stretch out on.

My family were keen to see how we were getting on and were among our first visitors. Happily they didn't have far to come. The new apartment was only about 400 metres from the house where I had been born and where my mum still lived. My dad's house was not much further in a slightly different direction. It felt good to be so close to my roots and I had to laugh at how the papers always said my old home was 'near the docks' while my new one 'overlooked the marina'. Same bit of water but a different spin to suit their stories.

Evidently Charlotte's parents had decided that they could no longer avoid the fact that their daughter's relationship was serious, so we got a visit from them as well. Amazingly, it went pretty well. One reason for the thaw, I suppose, was that their new hotel was doing OK, and Charlotte was enjoying going over there all the time, sometimes even helping out doing some of the rooms. She was the world's most famous and unlikely chambermaid, we joked.

Charlotte, meanwhile, no longer felt she had to live up to her parents' ambitions with every move she made. Or that she had to fit into the career box they had always built up for her. Everyone, for a while, was happy. Unfortunately Charlotte and I had long since learned one lesson about our crazy love affair. When we were happy, the media hated it and the papers twisted every fact to take the smiles off our faces.

That got proved one more time that summer. It was one of the lowest moments of my life, because in trying to do something good I was still accused of doing something really bad. Everyone around that night thought that I had done the decent thing, but one set of reporters took a completely different view. And my reputation as a bad boy and a troublemaker was sealed more than ever.

It happened one Saturday night in July when Charlotte and I were with my sister and a group of our friends at a club in London's Mayfair. It was a promotional night for the new album from Mr Cheeks, of rap star Li'l Kim fame, and it had been a great evening. Everyone had been drinking, dancing, having a brilliant night with music and people that we all respected and enjoyed. Charlotte and I were taking a break some time after 3am, trying to decide if we should head home, when we realised some trouble had broken out at the other end of the club. I felt my heart race when I saw that my twin sister Samira was right in the middle of it – and she was in danger.

A man – her ex-boyfriend, though I could only see him from behind through a crowd and didn't immediately recognise him – was grappling with her and they had almost fallen to the ground by the time security staff got to them and tried to pull them apart.

I threw down my glass and powered across the room to try and help. All I could see was my sister being pushed down, and as she went I got a glimpse of her terrified eyes. I joined the security guards, and tried to get the man's hands from my sister's throat. Had he hurt her? Had be been trying to kill her? Who would do that to a woman? I couldn't believe what we had just seen in those last few furious minutes.

Samira, being helped away by fellow guests and club staff, was crying to herself. I was almost doing the same, the adrenaline of seeing my twin in danger pumping through my body. And yes, all I felt was anger for this guy who had been fighting with her. In those first moments after they had been separated, I did take some swings at him – wouldn't you? – and glasses, tables and bottles went flying. Charlotte, who had become close to Samira, was at the edge of the crowd.

'I'll come with you,' she said as I headed back to her and said I needed to find my sister. When we did,

Samira was bleeding from several cuts on her face, she had deep red marks that would be serious bruises on her arms and she was crying heavily. We all headed downstairs at the club for some privacy, to try and find out what had happened.

'What happened?' I shouted, desperate to be heard above the blare of the music. 'Are you OK? Talk to us!'

'It all just happened so fast and I was on the floor. I thought he might kill me. I've never been so scared.'

We all tried to hold Samira and tell her it was over and that she was safe. 'Why, Samira? What made him kick off? Did someone say anything?'

Samira suddenly seemed to clam up and retreat into herself. Charlotte and I got frantic, convinced that she was concussed or something and I screamed at her to snap out of it and tell us she was OK. It was awful, just awful. When Samira finally told us to stop worrying we knew it was time to go home.

When Samira and her friends had left in a taxi, Charlotte and I got our coats and headed out the door. It had been a bad night – a party that had been so good had been ruined. I was still breathing deeply, the shock of what had happened still in my system.

'At least Samira is OK,' Charlotte said. 'She needn't ever see him again. It's over now.' But it wasn't.

The reporter with whom Samira had been talking decided to paint me as the bad guy.

'Her mum is said to despise him – and the sickening scene I witnessed in an exclusive London club will do nothing for Charlotte Church's case,' she wrote. 'I watched in horror as the millionaire singer's boyfriend Steven Johnson was caught up in a vicious brawl in front of a clearly terrified Charlotte. Saturday evening had started quietly enough. But by 3.30am things turned ugly. While the 17-year-old singer drank champagne with her DJ boyfriend, I chatted with his twin sister Samira. As we talked a young lad Samira said was an ex-boyfriend walked past us, turned and glared. "That's my ex and he's been doing my head in all night. He wants to get back with me, but I'm not interested," she told me. Suddenly the boy shouted: "Did she tell you that she's a lesbian?" before grabbing her by the arm. Then all hell broke loose. The boy spat at Samira, she spat back and the boy grabbed her by the throat. As security men struggled to separate them, Steven appeared and started throwing punches at his twin's ex – and anyone else within range. Glasses and bottles were sent crashing to the floor. As Charlotte stood by helplessly, bouncers restored some order, but not before Steven's sister was led away in tears, her arms and face bruised and bleeding. Steven had followed his sister downstairs – and got into a shouting match with her before the club heavies intervened. Thankfully, Charlotte and Steven left the club 30 minutes later. Over to you, Mrs Church.'

And that was it. From the article from the following day's *Daily Mirror*. I have to accept that it is pretty much factually correct. But how, out of that, can the man who leapt to defend his sister from end up as the bad guy? How can what happened that night show anything to Charlotte's mother except that her daughter would be safe with me?

But Charlotte and I knew, by now, that mud like this article was going to stick. It would also be repeated endlessly in any other article written about us. 'Film flops, family feuds and club brawls. Has the bubble burst for Charlotte?' headlined another paper a couple of days later. 'Just last week, thanks to her boyfriend, we saw another side of Charlotte's life – nightclub brawls,' it said, after suggesting that her career was on the skids. 'The *Welsh Daily Mirror* watched the fight unfold when Charlotte's "bit of rough" kicked-off last week as the pair attended a VIP party with friends and family.' So, as the truth trickled ever further away, it is suddenly described as if I just started a random fight to ruin Charlotte's night. And that is the way the story would be told in the papers ever since. Samira, not that anyone else seemed to care, didn't end up with any physical scars and has easily brushed off the whole incident.

Amazingly, one set of people who hadn't seen the events in Mayfair that July night were the BBC camera crew that was following us around for a year. Charlotte's managers were getting requests for interviews all the time – everyone seemed to want a few words from Charlotte on all sorts of subjects to help with documentaries, compilation shows or other programmes. If a crew would come out to Wales – and many wouldn't – and it was something Charlotte wanted to be part of, then she would normally agree. She also always gave good value when the cameras started rolling. This year-long 'fly on the wall' documentary of her life was in a completely different league, though.

At first no one thought it was a good idea. 'They'll edit it to make you look a bitch, or an idiot,' was one of the kinder comments we were given. 'No one ever wins on these shows – everyone who agrees to them always regrets it.'

But Charlotte, I think, was flattered by the attention, and having been stuck with the 'voice of an angel' label for so long, I think she also saw it as the best way to prove to people that the real Charlotte Church was very different. So, the BBC's *Spreading Her Wings* got the go-ahead. We first met the main writer and producer Christopher Terrill and his crew just before Charlotte's 17th birthday. The exact faces and names would change over the weeks and months, depending on who was available. But the two of us had to get used to the thought of having cameras around a huge amount of the time. And so did our friends and my family.

It was these other groups who perhaps should have been considered a bit more before the contracts were signed. I was a classic example of how an ordinary person can have their life turned upside down by being in the spotlight, so I could see why other people didn't want even a minor role in our little drama. The documentary got approved all the same, and filming had begun back in February.

I had said at the start that I didn't want to be filmed or interviewed on camera. I wasn't a celebrity; I was just a Cardiff lad with a famous girlfriend. Stuff like this made me nervous and seemed to take us even further from the relaxed good times we had when we were just an ordinary teenage couple behind closed doors. The media made both our lives a misery. I didn't see how inviting in even more coverage would help us.

Despite that, the crew did come along one day when I was having some new test shots done at my modelling agency. And with them, for the first time, came Charlotte. I was glad she finally saw me at work, and got to talk to the people I worked with. I hoped she'd realise that modelling wasn't all just me lying around with a bunch of beautiful women, and that she would relax a bit more about the work it was finding for me.

The rest of the summer saw us just relaxing and having fun. We were happy, and some people could obviously see that, because a bookmaker in Pontypridd actually started taking bets on us getting married in early 2004!

In the late summer my modelling agency also set up a series of photo-shoots for a big article in *OK!* magazine. It was going to be my first ever proper interview and I was desperate to get the chance to set the record straight about who I was, what I did and why I wasn't the tearaway that everyone thought I was. Going in the magazine on my own was a bit of a worry, though. I'd really wanted the two of us to do it together so we could explain a bit about how well our relationship worked behind closed doors and why we were happy together despite all the criticisms and bad publicity.

A joint interview and photo-shoot would also have been a lot more fun, but for some reason Charlotte and her management weren't up for it, even though they had given the go-ahead to the far more intrusive BBC documentary about her life. Anyway, I eventually sat down on my own to talk to the *OK!* people and tried to answer their questions. With a bit of luck I would finally be able to get my own personality across a bit. After spending time with me, the journalist Amanda Rimmer wrote: 'If ever there was a public figure whose reputation was built up around misconceptions then it's Steven Johnson. His bad-boy image just doesn't fit.'

We ran through loads of stuff about my relationship with Maria, my music and my modelling, as well as some of the stupid rumours about Charlotte getting pregnant. When that was over, the fun part of the day was the photographs. I had a load of my own clothes to wear, and the magazine had brought other ones as well – apparently that's normal for all those kind of celebrity shoots. Some people even get to take their favourites home with them, the make-up people told me, but I was too scared to do so in case it got in the papers and I got called a thief. To be honest, when they gave me a £3,500 coat for one of the shots I was almost too scared to pull it on in case I damaged it.

The magazine had booked an apartment in London's Covent Garden to do the pictures and, as on most model shoots, there were lots of staff buzzing around doing different jobs, and the styling and make-up people and the photographer were a real laugh. They wanted almost all of my pictures to be mean and moody, which wasn't always easy when we were having such a good time. But I think they ended up with what they wanted and seven of the shots made it into the final article, including two full-page pictures.

When the magazine finally got published at the end of September I couldn't believe that I had made it on to the cover, even though it was just in a tiny picture below the big one of, yes, Posh and Becks. This has to be the turning point, I thought. Surely the press can throw out all the dodgy pictures of me looking rough first thing in the morning or last thing at night and use these good ones instead? Surely they can see that I'm ready to make it on my own and I'm not with Charlotte for her money?

I had a lot of hope that September, and overall things were looking pretty good. The same week that OK! magazine was due to come out Charlotte had been asked to be a presenter at the MOBO Awards in London – proof that her new edgier and grown-up image was taking root. It was the eighth annual Music of Black Origin ceremony and after having the likes of

Destiny's Child perform in previous years it was set to be the highest-profile music event of the autumn. All of our favourite types of music were getting awards – including R&B, hip-hop, reggae, jazz, gospel, UK garage and world music. Justin Timberlake was supposed to be headlining the show. Mis-teeq and the Black Eyed Peas were performing, Li'l Kim was there and Christina Aguilera was up for best video.

The ceremony was being filmed for Channel Four and being broadcast live on the internet. It was a very, very big deal to be invited and we were over the moon to have the chance to be there.

We were also celebrating the fact that Charlotte's separation from her mother was over. The two were seeing each other a lot, getting on well again and that made everyone's life better. Probably as part of that, Charlotte's family had finally come around to the fact that we were aiming to stay together. Their acceptance was grudging, but it was better than nothing and we reckoned it gave us a sound foundation for the future.

'We hugely underestimated Charlotte's love for Steven. We had no idea her feelings were so strong,' Maria told a reporter that September when she was asked how she and her husband saw our relationship and how their family was getting along. 'Charlotte and I are great friends again and that is the main thing,' she continued. 'I have missed her so much. She has made some mistakes and so have I. I might not like Steven, but understand that for now he is part of her life. I just don't think he is the right one for her. I sincerely hope I am proved wrong because all I want is for my daughter to be happy. And at the moment I have to say she is extremely content.'

Charlotte was certainly content as we got ready for the big night at the Mobos, which were taking place at the Royal Albert Hall. We were staying at a Kensington hotel before the event and I have to say that even the rehearsals were a blast. There were so many faces that we recognised, so many people that we wanted to talk to.

Despite looking like a big night-time gig, it was still pretty light when we got out of our car at the edge of the Albert Hall. The last bit of the journey had been slow, because of all the other cars letting celebrities out in front of us. So we were pumped up by the time we got to the red carpet and climbed out. Charlotte was looking hot with very straight, newly blonde hair. She'd put a lot of black make-up round her eyes to draw even more attention to them, and was sexy but not uptight in a cropped, patterned black shirt and spray-on black trousers. I dressed down that day: I had picked a favourite pair of faded blue jeans and a pale, ice-blue sweater.

We held hands tightly as we edged up the carpet, an experience I don't think I'll ever get used to. There were way more fans there than we had expected and their reaction was amazing. People on both sides called out our names so they could get full-on photos. The press photographers wanted us to stay and pose for way longer than we'd expected.

Once inside the Albert Hall the atmosphere was even better. From the music world we saw Romeo from So Solid Crew, Jamelia, Lemar and Javine. George Benson was there, which would have made my dad happy. He was getting a lifetime achievement award on the night. America had loads of other stars there as well – rapper 50 Cent was one of them, and soul singer Blu Cantrell, who was co-hosting the show with Li'l Kim. Then there were all the non-music faces we spotted, like model Nell McAndrew and comedian Jimi Mistry. The whole thing was just brilliant and Charlotte and I were like two kids let loose in a sweet shop.

It was hot and stuffy where we were supposed to be sitting and so many people were just milling around that it looked as if the show would never get started properly. But we did finally get in place – Charlotte and I were sitting on a big round table right near the stage. When the show began there were loads of big surprises among the acts and the awards. Ms Dynamite made a last-minute arrival as a guest presenter and 50 Cent grabbed almost every award going. So was it glamour all the way? Not quite. Backstage before the awards began, I remember guarding a broken loo door to make sure Charlotte got some privacy while she was inside. Not exactly what you might expect at one of the show-business bashes of the year.

After the ceremony itself we headed over to the

after-show party, which was even better. I had spotted some of the producers I admired and I was hoping to get to talk to them. I'd also seen some seriously sexy women, including Heidi from Sugababes – but past experience told me that, while I was never going to touch, I had to be careful about even looking while Charlotte was around. Even with that hanging over my head, we both had a great night.

This was the kind of world where we enjoyed ourselves. Corporate gigs with Charlotte singing the stuff she had sung since she was 11 were not where we wanted to be any more, and that whole image, style of music and way of earning a living was about to get another kick towards the history books. Charlotte was planning a huge sort of 'goodbye to all that' concert in Hong Kong, and she wanted her family and friends there to see her do it.

CHAPTER FIFTEEN

GOODBYE ANGEL

Charlotte's career has been pretty amazing. Doubly so when you take into account that she did so much so young and in a field, classical music and opera, that is so far from the mainstream. It's easy for people to dismiss her, to just think about that one *Voice of an Angel* album and the one *Pie Jesu* song. But there's always been a lot more to Charlotte than that. She's travelled a lot of miles and done a lot of work to keep her profile high. Staying famous hasn't been an accident.

It's also pretty impressive that she has done so well around the world. The reception she gets abroad is often kinder and stronger than it is even in Cardiff, as she was to discover when she got booed at the city's Tsunami Relief concert at the start of 2005.

So Hong Kong in 2003 wasn't, in itself, a big deal for her. She had been there before, and when you look at the work she's done over the years she's been pretty much everywhere else as well. America, in particular, just loves her. She's a regular on all the big day and evening talk shows like Jay Leno, David Letterman and Oprah Winfrey, and if she has to she'll get up before dawn for the big American breakfast television shows as well. But all of that had been based around her old image and her old material. Hong Kong in 2003 was all about leaving that behind.

The hotel we stayed in was pretty much beyond belief. Our room was as high as it was huge and the views were incredible. Hong Kong itself was equally mind-blowing – the mass of skyscrapers crammed into such a tiny area with what seemed like millions of people rushing everywhere every minute of the day. The staff in the hotel were polite to the point of being embarrassing – it really seemed as if they would do anything for us.

But Charlotte was nervous and edgy. Something about the concert, or the place, or her plans, was bothering her, and for once she wouldn't tell me what it was. 'I'm fine, fine,' was all she would say. But I knew she wasn't.

We didn't sleep well that first night in Hong Kong, and as the bed was ridiculously big it was easy for there to be space between us. I didn't like that. I always hated it when Charlotte turned away from me to sleep at night. Did Charlotte have jet lag, a cold, worries about her material or the concert organisation? I never found out. But I wasn't the only one to be worried about her.

Charlotte had asked my sister Michaela to come along on the trip with us, so there would be more friendly faces in the wings on the big night. Mark and some people from her management company were also in Hong Kong with us for the three-day visit and the BBC's fly-on-the-wall documentary team were there as well. Charlotte and Michaela, who had always got on brilliantly and often went out on the town together at home when I wasn't around, were suddenly at each other's throats. Charlotte said Michaela was taking the piss by ordering too much from room service. I'll defend my sisters against anyone, but I hated having to defend one of them against my girlfriend.

In the end I remember I opened ten cans of Coke from the minibar just to make a point and threatened to get my ticket and fly home the next day. But deep down I knew Charlotte too well to do that. I knew she was picking stupid fights for a reason.

She was feeling insecure again – feelings that haunted her and could disappear and return at any time, for any reason. It could be because of the way she saw herself in a mirror one morning. The way another girl looked in a bar, a shop or a restaurant. The way a man did, or didn't, look at her. Any of these triggers and more could send her into a slump that seemed to last for longer and longer all the time. When we had first been dating I had been able to snap her out of her depressions by just holding and kissing her; by joking and laughing and telling her how sexy she was and how much I wanted her. Nearly two years on, the jokes were wearing a bit thin.

It was hot, humid and sweaty out on the streets of Hong Kong. Charlotte and I tried to lighten things up by doing some manic sightseeing. We went out in a tiny ferry across the harbour to try and get some air and we held hands wandering round some huge, crowded markets where we suddenly realised our usual roles were being reversed. Charlotte wasn't being recognised, so she was walking around without attracting a second glance. But with me it was the exact opposite – not because I was famous, but because I'm so tall. I towered over almost all the locals and they couldn't stop staring.

Walking around the hot and smelly bird market was another big memory of our sightseeing, though I wouldn't call it a high point. Both of us thought the tiny, overcrowded cages were cruel, and watching the birds being fed live bugs didn't seem much better. And did I mention the smell? If I ever end up in Hong Kong again I may give that place a miss.

Charlotte is a great shopper and so that took up a chunk of our time as well. Every top designer has flash air-conditioned stores in the huge underground malls there. But Charlotte wanted a bargain, so we stuck with the markets and with the BBC cameras on her she picked a rip-off Louis Vuitton handbag for about £20. A lot of people said later that this showed she's cheap as hell, but really it just proved she's just like anyone else, and I still liked that.

Unfortunately when we got back from our

sightseeing the bad atmosphere came back. Charlotte was far more nervous about this one-off concert than she had been about the ones in Hawaii or Las Vegas, so things were pretty tense backstage when they were doing her hair and make-up.

The hotel had put up a massive, white-tented city for the show. It was taking place in daylight but inside the tent it was dark. Charlotte looked fantastic when she finally hit the stage to massive applause. She started off singing one of her favourites, 'Tonight', and then ran through a lot of her usual numbers. I remember just watching her, mesmerised. Professional live performances are what I live to see, and Charlotte knows how to own a stage.

At the back of everybody's minds was the fact that this was a goodbye concert. It was being billed as the last time she would sing these types of songs – the last stage in her journey from under-the-thumb child star to fully independent adult. So when she took her bows, smiled and waved at the crowd after finishing off with 'Somewhere Over the Rainbow', we should have all been excited as hell. But somehow the mood wasn't like that. Everyone seemed subdued, and flying back from Hong Kong the next day wasn't a lot of fun.

The hotel had laid on huge cars to drive us out to the swanky new airport and were travelling in the big seats at the front of the plane again. But Charlotte was as nervous about takeoff and landing as ever – and for once I wasn't able to get through to her to comfort her.

Some weird barrier had come up between us. I didn't know why. I didn't know where it had come from or how long it would last. I didn't know if it was serious. All I knew was that Charlotte seemed somehow older. She was a little more tired, a lot more serious. And we seemed a long way apart.

The ride over the Severn Bridge didn't seem to improve Charlotte's mood, and we rattled around back in the apartment when we finally made it back to Cardiff. What bothered me most was that these ought to have been happy days. I was still over the moon with the way that the *OK!* magazine article had gone. I genuinely thought it was a turning point for me – which I thought should have made it a turning point for Charlotte as well. If I got some good new modelling work off the back of it and made some decent money, I could use that to set up a proper music studio in Cardiff. Charlotte and I could work there together, using the best talent we could find. It could be a new adventure for us both and I wanted to talk about it into the small hours like we used to do.

Charlotte, though, just wanted to sleep at nights, turning away from me in the process. At one point I even started to worry that she might be seeing someone else. I was sure that she wasn't, because that was something we had both said we would never do to each other – we would always be honest and talk to each other if we even thought of ever straying. Something, though, was suddenly eating away at the heart of our relationship. We were being hit from within, which seemed so weird and cruel and unfair considering we had survived so long when we were being attacked from outside.

What I didn't have, really, was anyone to turn to for advice. My dad was still down on Charlotte. He was convinced she was trying to stop my modelling career and just use me to get credibility as she tried to escape from the classical and opera world. My sister Michaela was no fan any more after the arguments in Hong Kong. It wasn't something I was going to discuss with my mates, and it didn't feel right to speak to Naomi or any of Charlotte's friends. Anyway, I told myself, it would probably blow over pretty soon. The old Charlotte would be back in a few days and I would just lick my wounds and wait until she did.

In the meantime, Charlotte had another job to do. She was finally going to give that speech at Oxford University, and that meant working out what she wanted to say and writing it all down. Considering what Charlotte had gone through since she had been about 11, and what we had both been through since we met, the obvious subject to talk about was the press and intrusion into people's private lives. It was something Charlotte had already spoken about a lot – including the previous winter after she had headed back to Cardiff instead of taking her flight to America to turn on the Atlanta Christmas lights.

'I know that when you kind of make yourself

available to be a celebrity you have to accept that certain parts of your personal life will be looked at,' she told ITN back then. 'That's OK for a 30-year-old who knows how to deal with things like that. But I think it's really sad how the papers distort a 16-year-old's life.' One year on, Charlotte had even more ammunition to attack the press. We spent a weekend just going through a whole load of newspaper articles to find examples she could mention and put in the slide show of headlines she wanted to use as a presentation. Some of them came from her management and PRs, who had collected everything. Some came from my dad, who'd kept some cuttings as well. And a huge amount came from Charlotte herself, who likes to read and keep as much of her coverage as possible.

It felt pretty strange to go through it all long after the event, as if the Charlotte Church and the Steven Johnson we read about were two completely different people to the ones in our big white Cardiff flat. On a few occasions time had healed some of the pain at the worst stories and we could almost laugh at some of the puns and jokey headlines. Other times, seeing a certain story just brought back all the anger or hurt or frustration we had felt at the time. The end result was that Charlotte was pumped up about the message she wanted to get across to the students in their anonymous lives, happily reading the articles that sometimes made hers so miserable. As she was going to be the youngest person ever to speak to the Oxford

Union, Charlotte knew there would be plenty of press coverage of the event – and she was hoping that at least some of the reporters might have an attack of conscience in the future.

So, off Charlotte went to Oxford with a bunch of her relatives. She rang me when they arrived, saying that the college was expecting around six hundred people in the audience, which would have put the fear of God into me. Before it all Charlotte was taken to some hotel for dinner with the Oxford top brass and star students; then they all got taken back to the college for a photo-shoot. I was worried that she wouldn't get much respect from the students, let alone the press that night. On her last phone call she had read out the biography of her that had been put in the information sheets for the event, and it pretty much just took the piss out of her. It didn't mention the millions of albums she had sold, or all the work she had done. Instead it just described her as 'The Welsh chorister who won the much coveted Rear of the Year at the tender age of 16'.

In the end Charlotte was in front of the students for around about an hour and a half. She ran through her argument that the press had to treat young people – and everyone else – better than it did, and she said she got some laughs by taking the piss out of some of the worst headlines.

Maybe we should have expected that when people decided to write about the event they ignored much of this, and focused on some of the answers Charlotte gave to the questions – none of which she had known about in advance. Thankfully she didn't have an answer when she was asked whether she would prefer to give up singing or sex, because I think that would have got on to the front pages whatever she had said. But she did have an answer when someone asked her to name any singers she didn't rate – her verdict was Victoria Beckham, which made everybody laugh and got Charlotte into the gossip columns again.

Her serious message – asking for proper privacy laws for the under-18s – was pretty much missed, but for Charlotte it had been another achievement. Back at home her mood hadn't improved much, though, and we found ourselves going out with separate friends a bit more. Whenever we had done that in the past we had made sure we met up at the end of an evening. That didn't always happen that November. Little things started to niggle at both of us. We didn't seem to laugh or joke as much. And we had stopped talking about the future. Maybe I'll never know what triggered all this, but something, somehow, had obviously gone wrong.

One area where we were arguing was on the music front. As I said, we had been working together since we met, playing around with lyrics and melodies, talking through people we would like to work with, tracks we would like to make. As we got more serious about all this, we had actually started some recording in the studio with one of the sound engineers I knew really well and trusted. In the end we worked on three main tracks and finished two of them. As I had a pretty decent studio set up at my mum's house, we were able to work from there as well as in the main studio, and it was good to have this secret project that no one else knew about.

What we were mainly interested in (and spent most of our time on) were dance tracks – and, if I say so myself, they worked. Charlotte's lyrics and her voice fitted the music, even though you might have thought that they wouldn't. She had an urban, edgy sound that would have surprised anyone who only knew her classical stuff. Both of us were proud of the end result when we listened to it. But that seemed to be as far as it went.

I sat in on one meeting Charlotte had with Sony, her record label. She had a copy of our work in her bag and was going to hand it over at the end of the meeting so we could start the process of possibly having it released. But in the end that didn't happen. The demo stayed in her bag as everyone shook hands and said goodbye.

'What happened to our demo? Why didn't you give it to them?'

'It just wasn't the right time. It wouldn't have worked,' Charlotte said afterwards. But I never really knew why or what she meant.

The whole subject came back up again in the apartment towards the end of 2003. After making the

Top Three with 'The Opera Song' earlier in the year, I thought Charlotte should have followed things up. She had two other similar tracks ready to release, as well as the work we had done together. I kept saying she was losing momentum and should get back out there. Yes, I wanted my work to be out there as well. But it didn't happen. And I got a real shock one morning when I opened my post and got a legal letter from Charlotte's management saying that if I ever released the tracks myself without their authorisation they would go to court to sue me.

Doors seemed to be closing all around on our relationship. Less than a year ago this sort of thing would have been something we would have talked over and sorted out together. Now I was getting letters from her management. It all seemed eerily familiar to the endgame for her first manager Jonathan Shalit, who was famously sacked in a letter sent by second-class post nearly four years earlier.

If I had thought all of this through properly, I would have seen the writing was on the wall for us. And I don't mean the 'I love Charlotte more than anything else in the world' that she had painted on the bedroom wall back at my dad's house. The words were still there, even though those days and nights suddenly seemed a long way away. But I still had hopes that we could bring them back.

CHAPTER SIXTEEN

GOODBYE CHARLOTTE

So why, when and how did it all go wrong? To this day it is still hard to say, exactly. But I remember I was on a train to London for a modelling shoot when I first realised that things had gone past the point of no return.

Charlotte had a morning meeting in London the same day and normally we would have made plans to catch up and maybe go out when we were both finished work. That day we hadn't. We weren't even travelling to London together. Charlotte had offered some reason about timings, or locations, or something that didn't really seem to make sense. But the end result was that she was being driven up in her car, while I was on the train. It gave me plenty of time to think.

The shoot I was heading for was for an American magazine and was taking place in Luton. There were going to be dozens of models there, and I was over the moon about getting the job with them. The shoot turned out to last a lot longer than I had thought, and it was the middle of the evening before I was free to leave. I rang Charlotte and got her answering machine. On a high after such a good day, I was desperate to talk to someone, so I rang a mate to brag about the models I'd spent the day with. After I had jokingly tried to make him jealous, he told me he had some news for me. Charlotte was back in Cardiff already. She was in the apartment. And she was having a bit of a party with a load of other guys there.

I didn't seriously worry that Charlotte might be cheating on me, not least because I knew she would never get away with it. Cardiff is a small place, and everyone knows everyone and everything about each other. I'd just found out that she was having a party, so there was no way it could be kept a secret if she was kissing another bloke. Or worse.

But one extra fact that my mate passed on did get me worried. He said someone called Kyle Johnson was there and that set a whole lot of warning bells off in my head. 'Kyle Johnson' was the same name as the guy who ran off with my first real love just before I met Charlotte. She had always been insecure about this other woman in my life, wanting to know who was sexier, slimmer, the better kisser, best in bed. And she had always wanted to know all the details of why we had split up and what Kyle Johnson's role had been in it all.

Was it crazy of me to think, sitting alone on that train, that one Kyle Johnson had stolen my first love and that another one was about to steal my second? And was it crazy of me to think that Charlotte would know this and might be setting something up to trigger some massive row? Whatever the truth was, we did have the big row.

By the time I got back to Cardiff the party was over and it was just Charlotte in the flat. But I'd already had more bad news. Another mate had rung me – a rumour was going around saying that Charlotte had actually been seen kissing Kyle. I told myself again and again that this was just stupid talk from people trying to cause trouble. But once I had that picture in my head it was hard to shake it off. Charlotte denied it all. Sure, she'd had some mates round for a party, she said. She'd do it again if she wanted to, she said. But she didn't want to talk about it, and she certainly wasn't going to talk about Kyle Johnson. We had a stormy night that night, two people in the same home but miles apart. But I still hoped that it didn't necessarily mean the end of our relationship.

What I hoped for was that it would be the old Charlotte who woke up the next morning. The one with the dirty laugh who would take the piss out of the rest of the world with me, and plan how we could build our lives together despite all the pressures. What I got, though, was this new, quiet and distant Charlotte again. The old days at weekends when we would just wake up at about 11, toss for who would make some bacon sandwiches, then slob around watching television, seemed a long way away. We ate separately and pretty much in silence that weekend.

And all the time I just couldn't work out what had changed. Was it me, I kept wondering? Was it the fact that I had been on another model shoot? Did Charlotte think something had happened between me and one of the models? The whole thing seemed so stupid. Charlotte had done enough shoots in her time to know they're just a mix of the frenzied busy and the deadly boring. She knows about the competition in that kind of world, and how it's just like Cardiff in a way. Models gossip like crazy, so if two of them get off together everyone will know it. A secret affair would have been pretty much impossible for me, even if I had wanted one. As the evening came I still believed that we could get back on track.

'You want to go out?'

We had been cooped up and miserable all day – it was December and it felt grey and depressing rather than Christmassy and exciting. Maybe it's a seasonal thing, I suddenly thought. A year ago there had been all the trouble at the airport when Charlotte had been so angry that I couldn't travel with her. Perhaps we would sort things out by Christmas, just like we had last time. And I'd better just get ready for another low at the same time every year.

But Charlotte didn't want to go out that night and her refusal was kind of like a challenge. Would I stay in too, so we could both pretend to watch television and carry on feeling miserable? Or would I go out with our mates anyway and leave her to stew?

Maybe I did the wrong thing. Maybe I wasn't a gentleman that night. But I went out with the gang – and deep down I hoped she would stew. I hoped she would be miserable in the flat on her own. I hoped that would help her snap out of all her depression and insecurity. Of course, as it turned out, I hoped wrong.

The lads and I all had a decent night out, a bit of drinking, a bit of dancing, some good music and good company. Charlotte should be here, I kept thinking. These are her people, this is her scene as well. What the hell is the matter with her and why doesn't she just forget what's bothering her and come over and join us?

When I got home in the early hours I found out what the latest problem was. Two days ago I had been told a rumour that Charlotte had been seen kissing someone else and I'd shrugged it off. Tonight someone had rung Charlotte up and told her that I'd been seen kissing another woman. She hadn't shrugged it off and she hadn't just been at home stewing. She had been at home building up steam, so when I put my key in the door she was ready to go ballistic.

'You bastard,' was the clean, printable version of what she said. And she said it again and again and again.

'What the hell is going on? Calm down!' That's the printable version of what I said back to her.

I tried to walk into the living room but she wouldn't let me. She blocked my way just inside the door, starting to batter me with her arms and her fists. I'm a lot taller than Charlotte, so she couldn't reach my face, though she seemed to be trying. I stretched out my arms to fend her off and hold her away.

'What the hell's the matter with you?' I screamed again.

'You bastard! How could you do this to me?'

Charlotte was crying now. Big tears, heavy breathing. I hoped the neighbours couldn't hear and kept on asking what was going on. In the end she told me. One of her drivers, of all people, had said he'd been told by his girlfriend that I had been kissing someone in a nightclub. First it was supposed to have been an air stewardess. Then a model. Then someone we both knew. As Charlotte forced the words out, the details kept changing. I was almost laughing with incredulity.

'But I've been with everybody all night. You know who I've been with,' I kept saying. 'You know where I've been. You were invited – I wanted you there with us all, you could have come.'

It didn't help. Charlotte couldn't be persuaded. She had heard a rumour, seemed desperate to believe it and was holding on to it for dear life. She was also bringing up all the other similar incidents of the past few months that had driven her wild at the time. The night when I had kissed one of my cousins goodbye in a club – when Charlotte had thought I was cheating on her. The night I had chatted to two women who wanted to do some recording down at the studio – when Charlotte had thought I was cheating on her. The night when I'd wanted to have some drinks with Christina Aguilera in London, for God's sake, when Charlotte seemed to think I wanted to cheat on her. I never had and I never did. But that night the list of accusations went on.

We both did a lot of thinking, I suppose, when things calmed down. And suddenly, just before dawn that night, I realised we had come to the end of our road. Charlotte, I realised, wanted it to be over. I didn't know why, but she did. And this stupid rumour was to be the reason.

I should have been angry. A few months earlier I would have been. But I wasn't. Maybe I hadn't quite realised myself just how much pressure had been building up these last few months. Maybe I hadn't seen that the pair of us couldn't beat the system. That two people can't stay together if the whole world seems to want them to be apart. The thought of walking away suddenly seemed the biggest relief in the world. It would mean an end to all the crap, all the worries about being judged, about how every action or word would be reported. It would mean being ordinary again. Just a bloke in South Wales trying to make it in the world alongside everyone else. Without having a time bomb at his side, always primed and ready to explode. I think I probably smiled, after a while, that night. It was all happening so fast. We seemed to have been so happy. Everything was fine. Then, in one night, everything was over.

Later on Charlotte would say that she convinced herself that the rumours about me supposedly having an affair must have been true because I had stopped protesting my innocence. She said that the fact that I didn't beg for forgiveness or plead for one more chance meant that I was guilty as hell. But in reality I had nothing to beg or plead for, and at that point I was as tired as a dog. That's why I decided to cut my losses and walk away.

Moving on meant moving out, however, and that was never going to be easy. Charlotte and I had both wanted this apartment to be a refuge, a home for the future, so pulling it apart and separating our stuff was tough. I started the job the next day – there didn't seem any point in delaying and there didn't seem much left to say between us. I didn't want us to close down completely and never speak or see each other again, and in the back of my mind I still thought this could all be just temporary. But we both knew it made no sense to talk that day. I got as much of my kit in bags as possible and drove it back to my dad's, back to where our relationship had first begun.

Meanwhile, Charlotte had a load of stuff over at my mum's, where we had spent a lot of time over the past few years. So she headed over there to collect it – not a pleasant experience for her, or my mum. Everyone wanted to know what was happening and why. I didn't have any easy answers, so I went out for a few drinks with some mates.

Later that night a group of us headed back to the apartment to get the last of my bags but Charlotte, for some reason, wouldn't let us in. For the first time I think I panicked then and thought that maybe she was having an affair. Maybe the guy – Kyle, or whoever it might be – was in the flat with her right then. After feeling sad, relieved and numb over the past 24 hours, I suddenly felt angry.

'Let us in, Charlotte. What are you doing in there?'

I remember shouting, screaming at her from the street. It suddenly mattered more than anything that I got into our home and checked that she was alone. I no longer gave a toss about my stuff. I just wanted to make sure I wasn't being made a fool of by the woman I'd loved. But Charlotte wouldn't let me in. The neighbours started to get involved and the whole thing threatened to get ugly, so we all headed off back to the pub. I needed a drink and some time to get my head together.

The one thing I could never believe, and still can't, is that Charlotte could have been genuinely scared of me. Yes, I was angry and I was shouting, but so was she. And Charlotte of all people knew that I defended women, I didn't attack them. So I just froze a couple of days later when I read the way that night had been described to reporters. The press, of course, went on a feeding frenzy when they found out that Charlotte and I had split up. All my family, my friends, everyone even vaguely connected with us was called up, approached or left notes asking for any information they could give. Big money was put on a lot of tables to try and persuade them.

Wherever they came from – and it obviously wasn't from any of my friends or family – the stories came thick and fast. Perhaps they were just invented in London and no one on Charlotte's side of the fence started spinning. Perhaps. Anyway, it began with the idea that 'Charlotte had to call security guards and police when Johnson turned up with a gang of friends at their former Cardiff home in the early hours.' Well, yes, I was with friends that night. I was with *our* friends, people Charlotte knew well and had spent so many good times with over the past few years. And the story of me trying to collect my final few bags from the flat that night was to grow and grow.

'Terrified Charlotte Church moved out of her luxury flat yesterday after a chilling death threat from her ex-boyfriend,' was the next bizarre version of it. It continued: 'Charlotte feared for her life when Steven Johnson turned up with pals at her Cardiff apartment and threatened to kill her.' It was amazing. Madness. Depressing. It just didn't resemble any of the events that actually happened and it just seemed to make everything worse. The papers, of course, weren't going to let it go and everyone but the Johnsons seemed happy to talk about our break-up. 'He cheated on me so I decided to give him the old heave-ho,' was one quote I read but failed to recognise as the real

Charlotte. But this was nothing compared to the stuff I read from her mother.

'Steven Johnson did not work for 18 months and leeched off my daughter. He is just upset because he has lost his golden goose, Charlotte,' was an awful couple of lines from Maria. 'Charlotte is very upset and it hurts me so much that he has hurt her like this. I have never liked him, but she loved him so much. Most women have their hearts broken and it is not very nice. Charlotte is absolutely devastated,' she said later, when asked to explain how her daughter was feeling.

The overall coverage was pretty terrible. Several of the articles went on about the 'constant rowing' that had characterised our relationship. It was the first I'd heard of it. Amazingly, a year after we had proved these stories wrong, they even dredged up and reprinted all this stuff about Charlotte buying me the £40,000 BMW as well as 'countless designer outfits'. Again, that was news to me.

The final one, which almost made me laugh, was the paper that wrote, 'Charlotte is said to have spent hundreds of thousands of pounds on him, buying him a sports BMW with designer number plates, plus countless designer outfits and holidays.' Bloody hell, I thought, if that were true she'd probably have to have bought me a whole new house as well to keep the 'hundreds of thousands of pounds' of kit in. Just where do figures and statements like that come from? Unbelievable.

Where I went wrong this time, just as I had done at

the beginning of my relationship with Charlotte, was trying to act all Jack the Lad and show off to the press. They were outside my mum and my dad's houses all the time again, knocking on the door, pushing envelopes through asking for interviews, offering the earth. 'This family doesn't intend to say a word,' my mum told one set of reporters, to try and calm them down and make them leave. But they didn't.

'Steven, what's going on with you and Charlotte? Is it true that you've split up?'

'Where are you both living now?'

'Is Charlotte with you, Steve?'

'What was the row about, Steven? Do you want to do an interview?'

The questions came like machine-gun fire whenever I left the house, the reporters pushing tape recorders towards me. Mostly I tried to keep quiet. I wasn't sure exactly what was going on myself. How could I tell anyone else? But one day I did lose my cool a bit.

'Steven, did you cheat on Charlotte? Are you seeing someone else? Will the two of you be getting back together?'

So I turned round and I said it. 'I'm with someone new now. She's a model. You'll find out who she is soon enough.'

That, I think, was what turned me from the papers' favourite bad boy and thug into their favourite love rat and supposed two-timer. One reporter called me 'Charlotte Church's utter tosspot of an ex', another came up with 'Steven rougher-than-a-badger's-arse Johnson', while one left it at 'a cheating creep'. But there never was anyone new for me. There never was any model. I'd just said it to try and show off, salvage some of my pride and get the reporters off my back for a few minutes.

Things didn't seem to be so clear-cut for Charlotte, though. I was being eaten up thinking that she might be with Kyle – and that their relationship might have begun before ours ended. Lots of rumours were swirling around saying that he had been going round to our old flat and that they had been seen out on the town together. Then, before anyone knew the truth, she headed off to spend Christmas in St Lucia with her mum and dad and I read that she'd become an item with a guy called Ed Foy who, the papers said, was a millionaire's son studying at Oxford. Considering what I knew about the papers, I didn't believe it for a moment. Maybe Charlotte had sat next to this guy in a bar, maybe even had a meal with him. But I refused to believe it had turned into anything more. I knew Charlotte too well for that.

What I didn't know about, still, was what was happening with Kyle. I knew who he was. He was 18 and I think he was working in a hotel somewhere in the city. I couldn't think what he might have in common with Charlotte. We had always had our music, the subject that kept us up talking late into the night. With Kyle it might be something different but I had no idea what.

In the middle of December I got a call through my model agency saying that *OK!* magazine wanted to do a big new photo-shoot with me. The good news was that, apart from the money, I would get some great new shots for my portfolio that might attract some interest from fashion clients. The bad news was that they wanted me to do an interview as well – and the main subject, of course, would be Charlotte Church and our break-up.

'Do it son, get the pictures taken. Show the world what you look like,' was my dad's response. He was determined that I shouldn't let my modelling slip now I was free to do any of the shoots I wanted. So in the end I went for it. We did most of the pictures in a flash apartment in London's Docklands, where the views stretched out towards the Millennium Dome. Despite feeling pretty miserable about life, the universe and everything, it was a decent day that helped pick me up a little. The interview itself was painful, though. The reporter, Ali Wick, was dead nice, and said I was completely different to what everyone on the shoot had been expecting.

'To those who don't know Steven Johnson, the former boyfriend of Charlotte Church, they might be forgiven for thinking he's a bad-boy Romeo with a sultry exterior and a talent for heart-breaking. Yet it only takes two minutes in his company to realise that almost everything that's been said about him is completely unfounded. Steven is, as a mother would say, a lovely boy who is painfully shy – perhaps so much that it is sometimes mistaken for arrogance. He's also incredibly polite and, instead of darting out of the door straight after our interview, shakes hands with everyone politely and says his farewells,' the article began.

When the magazine came out the cover was a bit of a shock. Jade Goody was the main picture on the front, but you couldn't miss my headline, either. 'I want Charlotte to take me back: World Exclusive interview and pictures. Her ex-lover Steven Johnson opens his heart for the first time,' it said, alongside one of the new pictures of me lying back on a bed looking miserable. Did I really say all that? I can't really remember. I hadn't taken the work in order to do the interview, anyway – for me it was all about the pictures, and as they looked pretty decent I was hoping they might open some doors again.

New Year 2004 wasn't a good time. Separate and separated, it was hard to suddenly be apart from someone who had been such a big part of your life for so long. Someone you had made plans with. Someone you had loved. Will anyone believe me if I say that I did wish Charlotte well back then? And that I still do today? Well, it's the truth.

Back in those bad few weeks after our break-up I did read one thing which made me fear that Charlotte had some terrible times ahead. As usual it was her mother who had said it. She compared Charlotte and me to

Kylie Minogue and James Gooding, who had also just had a high-profile split. 'Kylie received a wave of public sympathy and her career really took off. I can only hope the same thing happens to Charlotte,' said her mum. I couldn't believe it. It looked like the girl I had loved, the one who I knew craved freedom, was being put straight back on the career treadmill – broken heart or no broken heart. That's when I really felt sorry for Charlotte.

CHAPTER SEVENTEEN
SEPARATE LIVES

Picking up the pieces that January wasn't easy, because memories of Charlotte and our time together were absolutely everywhere. An old friend of mine, Tamzin Proctor, was trying to shake me out of my depression. A little while back, when Tamzin had split up with the footballer Sol Campbell, I had tried to cheer her up and show her life could still go on. Now she was returning the favour.

Tamzin had been the one who had first got me into modelling, when she'd asked me to take part in the charity fashion show in a Cardiff hotel. Since then her career had been really successful. She'd been a finalist in Miss Wales and done lots of big campaigns in magazines and on television. So she invited me up to stay with her in London for a few days, thinking a change of scene would do me good. She was a great shoulder to cry on. Tamzin is one of those rare people who really listens, who lets you talk and can help you see problems in different ways and maybe start solving them. We did get close around that time and I'll always thank her for that.

But Tamzin didn't think that just talking things through would get me over Charlotte. She thought a good night out would help as well. That's how we both ended up at the massive party at the Rex Cinema and Bar to celebrate Justin Timberlake's UK tour and, for the start of the evening at least, Tamzin was right. Loads of models, agents and photographers I knew from Select and various shoots were there, so there were masses of friendly faces around. That helped me feel better. It made me feel I still fitted in somewhere.

But then we saw Charlotte. It was one of those bizarre 'of all the bars in all the world' moments you just can't believe. Charlotte was at the same party. And she was heading our way. I suppose it had always been a possibility she would have been there – it was our shared music scene, after all, but I just hadn't thought about it. So Tamzin and I tried to act cool as Charlotte approached. I think she was on the way to the loo, and we were sitting chatting in a booth. And then it happened. She fell over. She actually slipped up on a canapé on the floor, people tell me, but whatever caused it, she ended up on her arse in front of us. Even now I have to say that it was funny. I did laugh, but it couldn't really have been more embarrassing for Charlotte. The whole thing was like some scene from a comedy film. No one could really believe it was happening and I still cringe for Charlotte when I think of it to this day.

At the time, though, things were pretty tense between us. That's why I was probably slow to move to help Charlotte get up and why the whole evening passed in a bit of a blur. Tamzin, though, had proved herself to be a true friend to me and I hate the fact that she got dragged down in the aftermath of my relationship with Charlotte. Over the next few days she was called all sorts of names in the papers. They said our friendship was just a publicity stunt, that we were cousins, that we were only together to try and make Charlotte unhappy. In the end it drove us apart, as well – another great friendship lost, albeit temporarily.

'The papers have ripped me to pieces and so many lies have gone into them,' Tamzin said afterwards. 'Nothing has been nice at all. It's been horrible, really hard to deal with and it's unfair on my family as well. My mum's had people banging on her door. It's upsetting and it just can't get any worse.' But, of course, it could.

My priority at this point was to pick myself up and focus on work. So I got back on the phone to Select to see how things had worked out on some of the jobs they had been talking about before Christmas. I was sitting on the end of my bed at my dad's house, Charlotte's writing still on the wall in front of me, when they told me the bad news. 'We think you need to take a break,' they said. 'Maybe get away for a few weeks till all this has calmed down. We can't book you as a model at the moment because of all the bad publicity about the break-up. Everything is about your private life and we need to get away from that. It's going to take some time.' I sat in my room on my own for a while after putting down the phone. Doors were closing again and I was going to have to start pushing some back open.

A week later, Charlotte celebrated her 18th birthday. These were sad times, really, because we had officially begun our relationship on her birthday, so it would have been an anniversary for us as well as her coming of age. But that year in particular, 2004, I went out with some other friends secretly relieved I wasn't with Charlotte. I was relieved because this year Charlotte got full access to her money, and it showed once and for all that I hadn't ever been after her for her money.

'Steven has lost his golden goose,' Charlotte's mum had said of me in that earlier interview just after the split. But if Charlotte had ever been my golden goose, then I wouldn't have let us just walk away from each other a matter of weeks before she came into her fortune. After February 2004 she would have been free to buy me a £40,000 BMW if she had wanted to – and to insure it. She would have been free to buy me the £20,000 diamond ring the papers said she had bought just before Christmas and taken back to a shop after our split. We would have been free to get married and I could have maybe claimed half of all she had, for God's sake.

If I had wanted any of those things I would have stuck around, I would have begged Charlotte to give us a second try, I would have refused to give up on our relationship. The fact that I didn't do any of this surely proves that all I ever wanted was the old Charlotte, the fun relaxed one with the dirty laugh and the same amount of money in her pocket as all my other mates. The money, quite simply, had never mattered one bit.

Perhaps because of the money, Charlotte's 18th birthday was big news and two high-profile television shows were being shown just after it to capitalise on the interest.

First up was a Channel Four show, *The Real Charlotte Church*. The producers had approached me to be in it just after Charlotte and I had split up, and as usual I said no. It all felt too raw to expose and talk about on television. But the requests kept coming, and I was pretty impressed by the status of all the other people who had agreed to go on the show. Charlotte's first manager, Jonathan Shalit, who I respected a lot, was on board, so were some of the top executives at Sony, some big opera critics, publicity experts and agents. But I still wasn't sure if I should agree or not. Then I was told that Charlotte's mum had said no to them, so on the spur of the moment I said yes.

We only did a couple of hours of filming. I sat in front of the cameras and they asked me about the break-up and what I thought about the way the media had pursued us both. I didn't know if all or any of it would make it into the final programme, but it was done really professionally and wasn't as terrifying as I'd feared.

After that show had aired, next in line was the result of all the fly-on-the-wall filming that the BBC had been doing since Charlotte's last birthday and which had carried on after our split and into the New Year. *Charlotte Church: Spreading Her Wings* was 'pick of the day' in most newspapers when it was finally broadcast, and my dad, sisters and I watched it pretty much in shock.

The good stuff came first. 'Steven is always at her side, they're pretty much inseparable,' said Rhiannon Meades, the narrator, when she started describing Charlotte's crazy year. Kim from Select was also on to give her verdict on us both on the day Charlotte came round to the agency to watch them do some test shots of me. 'I'd never met Charlotte before until she came here today, but they seem very in love. It's nice,' she said. And it was – at least back then.

What the early part of the documentary showed was just how much Charlotte's mum protected her and did her planning for her. 'Everything was fine until I met Steven and when I met Steven she just lost it,' Charlotte said about Maria. 'She's never trusted anyone around me, not even my friends. It's not just Steven she's not liked, she's really paranoid that they're all going to sell out on me.'

What made me happy was the fact that Charlotte had the guts to fight back against her mum on camera.

'The fact is that she's very fond of Steven,' began Maria at one point.

'I love him,' interrupted Charlotte, furious at her mother. 'And he loves me.'

But still Maria refused to accept it, making some comment about everyone being young once and making a face at the camera.

Later on, in the parts filmed after we had split up, Charlotte was still trying to be realistic and reasonable, while her mum was still going off on one.

'I have no respect or loyalty for his family. I don't like them,' Maria declared.

'You don't know them,' Charlotte pointed out.

'I don't care,' was all her mum would say.

Then, worst of all, was the bizarre stuff about Charlotte supposedly being moved into a safe house in the dead of night because of death threats. This was where my family watched in complete horror and disbelief, and where I lost respect for the producers. The whole thing was ramped up into something really frightening and then Charlotte went on camera to say that it had been nothing of the sort. So why had the producers shown it in the first place?

It began when Charlotte and her mum were shown looking around a house Charlotte was moving to where the electricity and the lights didn't work. This meant they explored it by torchlight, making everything seem sinister and dangerous. The commentary pretty much said that Charlotte had to be smuggled out of her old apartment in the dead of night and was being moved into this new place because of threats I had been making. But if things had really been like that, surely they would have taken Charlotte to a hotel, to her parents' house, or left her safe behind the porters on the top floor of our old apartment block? And surely Charlotte and her mum wouldn't have been laughing and joking about the lack of lights if they were really in fear of her life?

All this was glossed over, though, and the show carried on trying to make everything look as dramatic as possible, giving the impression that I was the kind of man who would beat up an ex-girlfriend. To give her credit, Charlotte did defend me. All the claims about my alleged threats came from her mum – and one by one Charlotte shot them all down.

'He never threatened me, he never threatened anybody, he was just knocking on the door,' Charlotte said at one point about the night when I had come round to collect my things and move out. 'No, he never said that! What are you on about?' she asked when Maria carried on about the stuff I was supposed to have said.

'She looked terrified,' Maria then said to the camera, clutching at straws.

'I was fine!' Charlotte fired back.

But, as usual, the damage was done. The whole country had seen Charlotte apparently forced to go underground in the dead of night to find safe refuge from her thug of an ex-boyfriend. My reputation was right back in the gutter again. Maria had finally got her revenge on me and I'm sure she was over the moon about it.

Sadly, in the middle of all this badness, I lost another friendship that had started to mean a lot to me. I'd been quietly dating a local hairdresser, Emma, since the start of February, and while it was very early days we'd had some nice times together. Both of us had been through some bad times – she had actually been dating Kyle before he had got together with Charlotte – and so we had plenty to talk about. It was also great to be with someone who, apart from all that, was just good company and lived an ordinary life. But in the end the Charlotte and Kyle links got too much for us. Emma, I think, wanted to get away from all that, and was worried she was being used in some sort of revenge war or publicity battle. She wasn't, and I missed her when we stopped seeing each other.

What I wouldn't have missed was seeing so much of Charlotte and Kyle out on the town with each other. Because Charlotte and I had shared so many friends over the years it was tricky to avoid being in the same places and seeing the same people. I ached sometimes, wanting to speak to Charlotte, wanting to go back to the old, fun days. But when I tried to speak to her, something always got in the way or she made it clear that she didn't want to speak to me. Or, on other occasions, like the time that Charlotte saw my car outside a club and left her mates to come over and say hello, I suddenly felt I wasn't ready to speak to her and I drove away. It was a series of confusions, misunderstandings and missed opportunities – normal stuff when love affairs end, I suppose, but it made it all far harder to deal with.

It was early March, nearly three full months since Charlotte and I had split up. I was at home, watching television. And still reporters kept ringing up.

'How long is this going to go on for?' my dad asked, again and again, wanting his quiet life back. None of us knew. And I wasn't as wise and as clever about dealing with these calls as I should have been. I know I made mistakes back then that meant the nightmare would hang over me and my family for even longer.

One of them came when a paper called me and offered me some money for a photo. It wasn't for one of the private photos of Charlotte that I still guard carefully. It was to be a picture of me – stage-managed to look like a paparazzi shot. The *Big Brother* producers were in Cardiff auditioning for that year's set of housemates. The paper wanted me to go along, stand in the queue, pretend I didn't know I was being photographed and give them a nice picture story for the next day.

Why, exactly, did I say yes? I have no idea. It wasn't even as if they were offering much more than small change. But I wasn't doing anything else that day and for some reason it felt like it would be a bit of fun. It wasn't so funny when they ran the story, implying I was a sad media wannabe – and included a line from a 'Big Brother insider' saying I wasn't the kind of person they were looking for so I didn't stand a chance of getting on the show anyway. I should have seen that one coming.

I should also have had my wits about me a bit more the next time I saw Charlotte and Kyle together in public. It was less than a week after what would have been our anniversary, and all of us had been drinking a bit that night. I should have just headed away but I didn't. We were all at the Owain Glyndwr club in town and things kicked off just before closing time. I'd seen Charlotte and Kyle there all night and was getting ready to leave with some mates when Kyle left the club, and for some reason Charlotte wasn't with him. We started off like kids, calling each other names, all the usual stuff. Then, after months of build-up, it escalated into a scuffle. It wasn't a full fight, more like letting off steam, and, though I hadn't felt anything at the time, when I got home I saw I'd got a bit of cut below my right eye.

Next morning the phone rang. The papers had been told that something had happened and wanted all the details. In particular they wanted to know if I'd been hurt, and while it was sort of embarrassing I told them about my eye. Should I or shouldn't I have agreed? I don't know, but I did let a photographer in to get a picture. And another story got written making out I got into fights all the time. The papers that had started out saying I was a layabout from a bad part of town had moved on through calling me a parasite and a cheat to making out I was now practically a criminal.

'Stevie, you need to do something about this,' my dad kept saying. 'You need to get your side of the story out there. You've got to put the record straight before they destroy you completely.' He was right, as usual. But it was easier said than done and I was terrified of making matters worse.

The last time I had spoken to the *News of the World* everything had gone wrong. My mates and I had taken them up on their offer of some free drinks and a long afternoon in the St David's Hotel and had been badly burned. This time I decided it would be different. I would be in charge and I would use the interview to explain who I was and what I wanted to do with my future. Of course, my relationship with Charlotte was always going to be central to any story – I wasn't stupid enough to think Sunday newspaper readers would be interested in me alone. But I was determined not to fall into the kiss-and-tell trap. I wanted a contract, and in it I wanted to state quite clearly that I wouldn't talk about sex. In the future other people could spill the beans on what Charlotte was like in bed – that's what Kyle did less than a year later. But it wasn't my style and I wouldn't budge on the issue.

I took it very slowly when I finally spoke to the *News of the World* people. I was very nervous, and the reporters kept trying to push me to say more than I wanted to –

especially about private stuff – but I kept trying to stay on track. The interview only lasted for around an hour at most, and the reporters seemed to know exactly what they wanted me to say, so everything that happened was pretty much a formality. So after signing the contract we all said goodbye and I had to just sit back and wait till the weekend to see what they would write.

When Sunday came the final article didn't at first glance look like the romantic, forward-looking piece I had hoped for. But at least they hadn't made up anything horrible about sex or the personal stuff.

ANGEL'S SECRET NIGHTS OF SIN screamed the headline. 'In his first newspaper interview male model Steven Johnson told the *News of the World* all the secrets of the searing PASSION, insane JEALOUSY and fiery BUST-UPS that peppered their high profile affair.' But, while that obviously suggested I had broken my code and talked about sex, it just wasn't true.

I had clammed up almost totally whenever they had asked me about sex. So when they wanted to include details of the first time we had made love, the reporters were forced to fall back on a year-old quote from Charlotte that she had made to another magazine. All they got from me was: 'It was special. We were so happy. We even discussed getting married and having children we were that serious.' It was hardly 'searing passion', but at least I could hold my head up high.

And what about the 'angel's secret nights of sin' from the headline? That was my description of how

Charlotte would sneak out of her parents' house to come round to my dad's place for a cuddle – before getting a cab back to hers in the morning.

In the cold light of day it was pretty tame stuff and I think the *News of the World* people had struggled to sex it up. I also really hoped that Charlotte would see it that way. I hoped she would also see that, yes, I did do the interview for the money, as well as to try and put the record straight about my own life. Charlotte's a professional entertainer, and professional entertainers and celebrities give interviews for money all the time – sometimes including very personal ones. Charlotte had done just that when she had told a magazine all about losing her virginity to me well over a year before. So when I search my conscience I can't feel bad for having given a far less personal interview; especially as the repercussions of being at the centre of a media storm with Charlotte were still being felt.

First up, I got official news that my contract with Select in London wasn't being renewed. The agency was incredibly nice about it. They said great things – that they had always liked my work, my commitment and the effort I had put into it all. They liked my look and the way I photographed, but I had just become too closely associated with bad stuff. Clients didn't want to buy into all that by booking me. They wanted blank-canvas models who would take anything away or add anything to the client's main message. I needed a fresh start somewhere else.

Even worse was going on back in Cardiff. I was 19 years old at that point, and I had never been in trouble with the police in my life – until that spring, when it happened twice. First I got stopped in my car. It didn't seem a big deal because some mates and I were just sitting around killing time. I hadn't been speeding or drinking and I had full tax, insurance and everything else. The police, though, thought a group of guys in a car meant only two things – drugs or guns. Because I knew we didn't have either I was annoyed, but not that bothered, when they said they wanted to search the car. If they thought I was some kind of gangster then they would soon find out that they were wasting their time.

They didn't, of course, find any drugs or guns. But they did find something. It was a martial arts thing that belonged to another mate of mine who I'd helped move house a few weeks ago. Some of his stuff was still in my boot, including what I later found out later on was called a nunchakus. It's a kung-fu thing that Bruce Lee used to use in films and it's illegal in Britain. What I also found out was that it didn't seem to matter at that stage that the nunchakus wasn't mine. If it was in my car it was treated as in my keeping, so I got charged with possession. Suddenly I felt like a little kid again. My mum and dad would be furious, and I hated making them miserable like this because I know how much they worry about their kids.

Even more embarrassment and stress was to come in

a couple of months. It was May, the weather was good and I'd gone out to a friend's barbecue. Six months after saying goodbye to Charlotte, I was finally feeling ready to try and date seriously again and that day I spotted a girl I really fancied. She was one of my sister's mates and I was trying to catch her eye all afternoon. By the evening I knew I was getting somewhere and I was feeling pretty good. Pretty much everyone from the barbecue headed on into town in a big group. We hit our first club, the girls were there, and then suddenly it happened.

I had been recognised as Charlotte Church's ex – the supposed bad boy from the wrong side of town, who the papers had just said carried a dangerous weapon in his car. That, I knew, made me a target for any lad out there who wanted to prove how hard he was to his mates or his girlfriend. And so it started.

'Who the hell are you?' one guy started shouting at me, with a bit more colourful language. 'Who the hell do you think you are, anyway?'

'Nobody,' I wanted to say to him. 'I don't think I'm anybody special at all. I'm just a local lad you've read about and think you know. But I can pretty much promise you that most of the stuff you've read is wrong, so you don't know me at all.'

But of course I didn't say that. I told him where to go, my mates got involved, the girls were looking on and it all started going too fast. I tried to leave because I knew I would get hit with the blame if something serious kicked off, but I didn't get the chance. Something serious had kicked off and I was dragged into it. Like most club fights it was intense and frightening. Punches were thrown first, then glasses and bottles. Everybody around seemed pumped up and ready to join in, even if they didn't know who the hell I or anyone else was.

The police got called, of course, and when everyone was being pulled apart and sorted out I was one of the first ones arrested. I was up for Section 18 assault, something I didn't even know about until then. I spent what felt like for ever in a police cell, waiting for everything to be processed. The whole experience was unbelievable. I sat there, waiting and waiting to find out what was going on, thinking this just couldn't be happening to me. I couldn't see how my life had come to this. I couldn't see how the teenager who was into computers and music was now in a police cell.

The nightmare lasted for nearly a year before my trial came up before a jury. I'd actually ended up more injured in the fight than I'd thought – doctors say I'll never get full use of all my fingers again after one piece of glass slashed through some tendons. Two of the other guys who had been arrested with me were released without charge, but for some reason Steven Johnson, the one the papers had written about, was kept on the court list and could end up going down.

What I also couldn't believe was that I was still worth photographing when I finally came to court. The snappers were there again, wanting the pictures to illustrate a new set of stories – ones that would say I really was a bad boy and that they had been right all along.

Things didn't go smoothly even when the case finally did come up. One of the security guards in the court room saw one of the jury members making a V-sign and other gestures at me as I was in the dock. That got reported to the judge, who dismissed the jury, called a meeting of the lawyers, said there wasn't enough evidence against me anyway and then said I was free to go.

A whole year. Everything on hold. A massive shadow over everything that I did, and it ended without a single charge being proved against me. I was formally not guilty, which was the best news that me and my family could have been given. But, while I wanted to celebrate the news I was still being dragged down by what I knew was the biggest downside of having your name or your face in the public eye. People judge you and they decide they hate you, even though they don't even know you. They can form opinions on the basis of a single photograph, a few throwaway lines of quote or a judgement by a columnist. And as you go about your daily life, you never know when, or if, one of those people who hates you is going to serve you in a shop or a bar, pass you in the street or get introduced to you at a party. You never know when it might cause you a serious problem. Charlotte used to be driven mad worrying about this sort of thing. A year after we had split up, I finally knew exactly what she meant.

CHAPTER EIGHTEEN

THE OTHER SIDE
OF THE STORY

So far I have told my story of my life with Charlotte Church. I have tried to tell it like it was, remembering all the things that happened, in order, and put them all down on paper. I may have got one or two little things wrong, because I'm not the kind of person who keeps a diary, and dates and events do all blur over the years. But I've tried to say what happened to Charlotte and me, to explain what we did, what we thought and how we felt about things.

But the people around me – my family and the people who love me – saw a lot of things differently at the time. What they say is that there was always more going on than just two innocent teenagers fooling around, falling in love and trying to build a life together and that a lot of the bad publicity could have been avoided. When I'm feeling low I have to agree with some of them, though I fought against believing it at the time.

My dad was the first to ring warning bells, right after
Charlotte first started spending the night in our house.
He liked the girl who ran up the stairs to my room with
her friends, and then started appearing on her own at
his table. But Dad was worried. 'Rottweilers breed
Rottweilers,' he used to say. If she stayed the smiling,
relaxed, friendly girl I first brought home, then
everything was going to be fine. But if she began to
turn into her mother, which Dad thinks many women
do, then we were in deep trouble.

What worried Dad the most was not just that I had
been dubbed a 'bad boy' by the press but that no one
in Charlotte's world seemed to care. Could it be that
my 'bad boy' tag was actually good news for Charlotte's
career and that those around her had no reason to help
me shake it off? What Charlotte wanted so much at
that point was street credibility. She wanted to shake
off her child-star image and break into the adult market
– in dance music, R&B or whatever. But this was never
going to be easy for someone with such a wholesome
image, so Charlotte had to show the world she'd grown
up. She might have the voice of an angel, but she was
desperate to prove that she no longer acted like one.

In the early days when we were dating, I did think
that Charlotte got a buzz out of the publicity we got.
And that takes me right back to that photograph of
Charlotte smoking. As I said, Dad knew what would
happen if she walked out of our door with a cigarette
in her hand. He knew the papers would go wild and

that he and our house would get dragged into all the criticism. He asked her, told her to stub it out before leaving the house. But she wouldn't.

She had been in the public eye since she was a kid. She had seen how good news and bad was created and perpetuated. She knew what sold newspapers, what sold records and what sold concert tickets. I'd always reckoned Charlotte just didn't think straight that day. It was part of her rebellion, her revenge on her parents, and I didn't think she realised this would end up causing so many problems for me, my dad and our neighbours.

'Steve, you got to watch that girl. She'll drag you down with her,' my dad said – the exact opposite of what everyone else in the world seemed to be thinking. And looking back, Charlotte didn't really like me pulling myself up by getting into modelling, for example. She clammed up when I first told her about the phone calls suggesting I do some jobs. She hated the fact that a fashion designer sent me some of his clothes to wear in public. And she didn't like hanging around while I waited for casting sessions to finish, even though I did the same kind of thing for her.

Why was she was so unenthusiastic about my opportunities? Was it that she didn't want to share the limelight? Was she was worried that if I got work I would have to travel and not be able to chill out with her so much? Was it the thought of me being with female models who would be taller and slimmer than her? Probably it was all three – even though none were ever any kind of a threat to her. I don't think I could have made it more obvious to Charlotte that her body turned me on – especially her legs, which she wrongly thought were one of her worst features.

For all the great stuff that the modelling people had told me, I didn't flatter myself that I would be booked with top jobs seven days a week. I also didn't think that me making a name for myself in a career separate from Charlotte's music would do anything but boost our public profile. Charlotte appeared as unhappy as I was about all the newspapers referring to me as a 'thug' and a 'leech' and a 'scrounger'.

When my dad really lost it with Charlotte it was over the photo of her wearing the 'My Barbie is a Crack Whore' T-shirt. Her mum and dad were on the phone to her straight away saying she was risking her whole career by wearing something like that and asking her how she could have been so stupid. I had been put in touch with several major clients – including Rockport and Mercedes – about modelling work. They wanted my look to help sell their products but they didn't want any distractions.

Having my face on the front and features pages of every newspaper with my arm around a girl the papers said I was helping to destroy was about as distracting to their message as you could get. When I got back from America the meetings to represent those firms had been cancelled. They were reconsidering their campaigns, they said. They would get back to me, they said. But they didn't.

Being photographed with Charlotte wearing that t-shirt certainly didn't do me any favours. I carried on defending Charlotte to my dad and the rest of my family, and one night I got as many of them together at the house as I could to prove I was right. I wanted to get my sisters and their kids back on Charlotte's side because she had also pissed them off over something else.

Charlotte is a strange mixture of generosity and meanness, and it was the meanness that my sisters had spotted. For example, Charlotte had rung me from America just before Christmas 2002 saying she was in one of the giant Reebok stores and the manager said she could pick up as much kit as she wanted – so what did I need? There were loads of people in the house when she called and I didn't want to look like I was sponging off her, so I said I was fine. Once I'd done that I could hardly complain when she turned up back in our house with loads of free kit, which she handed out to all her mates. But a bit of me thought that if it had been the other way around I would have still got her something, however much she had said she didn't want it.

Then there was something else, too, something very small but which niggled away at people even more. Back then Charlotte spent a lot of time playing with my baby nieces and nephews and ate a lot of sweets. But the kids said she never shared the sweets with them. It's a tiny thing, but it had all added up to colour the way my family were starting to think of my girlfriend, which I didn't like at all.

Anyway, the night she was on telly was the night she could get back in everybody's good books. The occasion was a major ITN interview Charlotte was doing about her career and her future prospects. I had begged her to take care about how she described me and to try and get the message across that I was a decent bloke who worked hard and wasn't the person the tabloids liked to think I was. So me, Dad, my sisters and a few others all sat around our big television in Cardiff when the programme came on. I was convinced she wouldn't let me down. But we were all in for a big disappointment.

To give the full background, I had told Charlotte my agency had said I might get included in some multi-million-pound campaigns. Somehow, that figure ended up in the papers as how much I had been signed up for – even though it was ridiculous that a first-time model would even get close to that kind of money. And that, pretty much, was what Charlotte, who was normally such an expert in diplomacy, said on national television – that rumours of me having a £1.5 million modelling contract were complete rubbish. I felt humiliated that my girlfriend had just made me look so small. Dad was furious at what he saw as Charlotte's disloyalty.

So why did Charlotte act that way? After all, she knew exactly how to say the right thing at the right time; it was part of her job. There were plenty of other ways she could have put it more tactfully and more supportively. I reckon it must be something to do with all the insecurities in her head. What I do know is that it pretty much ended Charlotte's relationship with my dad, and that wasn't great news, as Charlotte was still living with me in Dad's house.

Charlotte stayed out of his sight for a couple of nights. We both went to my mum's instead but the atmosphere there was almost as frosty. Dad stayed mad, but as usual I gave Charlotte the benefit of the doubt. She said she hadn't realised the effect the interview would have on me, or the way people would interpret what she was saying. She said she was sorry if she had caused me any problems. She said that this was the last thing she would have wanted and that she supported me absolutely in everything I wanted to achieve. It was what I wanted to hear so I forgave her. There was a lot I wanted to achieve and I didn't want to get caught up in side-issues like these.

Then there was the fact that Charlotte never pushed our recordings or our ideas in her meetings with Sony. And then she certainly made sure I wasn't able to do anything with them on my own.

And while the press had written loads of stories saying I was out on the town till all hours while Charlotte sat alone wondering where I was, the exact opposite had started to happen. Charlotte's late nights with the girls started to get more frequent, and a lot of them seemed to coincide with the night before I had a casting or a photo-shoot, so I never got the sleep I needed to look my best. At this point some of the jobs I was up for were about as good as you can get – casting for New York Fashion Week, Hugo Boss, really big events and big money brands. I started to feel I was never able to prepare properly.

Throw in the fact that Charlotte refused to do joint interviews with me – despite repeated requests from *OK!*, *Hello* and other magazines and newspapers – and in retrospect I wonder why I didn't end up feeling even more isolated.

Even after we had split up, Charlotte's shadow turned out to be a long one. In those first few weeks of being apart I tried to keep my career on the road and thought my new *OK!* magazine photos were a great way to do it. I wasn't the only one. Apparently they got spotted by someone at Armani when they were about to cast a big new clothing campaign. Getting on board with a company like that would have lifted me into the premier league. But just as negotiations were about to get under way, someone leaked to the press the ridiculous story about me threatening Charlotte's life, and of her being forced to move into a 'safe house' for her own protection.

If you were about to spend big money on an important new campaign, would you want someone in it who might have done something like that? Didn't think so. And even though Charlotte finally shot down her mother's claims and said she had never been threatened by me or scared of me, the damage had been done. Armani had moved on and I was back where I had started.

Even now I'll buy the fact that all these things which affected me badly may well have happened without her really knowing what she was doing or what the consequences of her actions would be. On one television programme about Charlotte, the psychologist Oliver James had a lot to say about how she subconsciously did a lot of things purely and simply to get back at her parents and to hell with everyone else. Maybe I was just some of the collateral damage in this battle, even if she wasn't aware of it. But something always seemed to blow up or go wrong just before I ever got to take the next big step in my own career. If I have any regrets at all about my time with Charlotte, it is because of things like that.

CHAPTER NINETEEN

CHARLOTTE TODAY – AND TOMORROW

As I write this the girl I had first seen at a party when she was just 15 is nearly 20. And if you believe what you read in the papers – a bad joke – then she is out of control. Charlotte has been dating again, this time the Welsh rugby player Gavin Henson, whom her family seem to have adored from the off. 'I always said Charlotte should date another celebrity. That way they won't do another kiss-and-tell,' Maria was quoted as saying before turning up at a rugby match and parading for the cameras next to a group of 'We Love Gavin' T-shirts.

On the kiss-and-tell front, poor Charlotte has certainly suffered. I'm proud that I refused to talk about sex when I spoke to the *News of the World*. Kyle Johnson, the man she dated right after me, didn't feel the same, however. I was sitting at home with my dad and my sisters when we got the papers the Sunday his story was published. It really was pretty X-rated stuff. ANGEL

UNCOVERED: OUR NAKED LUST, THE FIRST CHURCH SERVICE AND THAT HEAVENLY BODY ran the headline. 'Great boobs, better bum than Kylie ... and she can make love till dawn.'

Like every other *News of the World* buyer that weekend, I couldn't stop myself from reading on. 'I've lived out the fantasy of millions of blokes – and you'd better believe Charlotte is as gorgeous naked as you'd think,' Kyle said. But he was also keen to point out how good he supposedly looked as well. 'She told me: "I think we have brilliant sex. Your body is so great and whenever I see you with your top off I really want to go to bed."' Yuk! But there was more to come.

'Charlotte knew all the tricks all right. It was every day and every night in every room of her flat – even the bathroom. We loved doing it in the shower with the hot water pouring down all over us. It was really horny. We wouldn't stop until we were totally knackered.'

Kyle went on to describe an £18,000 holiday Charlotte had treated him to, and again the focus was on what happened in the bedroom. 'We flew to the Maldives and stayed in a beach hut on stilts over the sea. That night we did it in the four-poster bed all night long and as I was on top I saw a baby shark swim beneath us through the floor boards. The whole setting was magic. I felt like I was in heaven.'

Reading this I thought he should go to hell – this was far too personal and sleazy and I could see how much it would hurt and embarrass Charlotte. I even felt like ringing her up to tell her I hoped she was OK and to just ignore it. But as it turned out, Charlotte was more than able to cope. Mates rang up to tell me about it within an hour of it happening, and it made the papers as well. Charlotte had seen Kyle at a late-night restaurant in Cardiff just after finding out about the article. She hadn't cried, she hadn't snuck out of the back door or bad-mouthed him behind his back. She went right up to Kyle, said a few words about how crap he was and punched him in the face! That's my girl, I thought. That's the girl I wish hadn't changed.

One thing I wished Charlotte was still doing, though, was her music. In the spring of 2003 I had kept asking why she wasn't releasing any of the follow-ups to 'The Opera Song', which had been such a big hit. She had never really been able to explain her thinking to me – or maybe she was being held back by her management and didn't want to talk about it. It seemed strange, though. She had proved she could cross over from the classical and opera world and she could have made more of a mark on the charts. Even if she decided to change course again afterwards, at least she would have had more behind her.

So I had pretty mixed feelings when I heard on the grapevine that she had recorded a track all about me after we'd split up. It was called 'Casualty of Love' and it wasn't very flattering. 'Mama was right' was supposed to be a big part of the chorus and, if some of the articles about the song were to be believed, there were other lyrics about coming from different classes and other bad stuff. Apparently Charlotte first sang it in public at the Lesbian and Gay Festival in Cardiff in the summer of 2004 and decided that, as it got such a good reaction, it should be released as a single. That idea soon got knocked on the head, fortunately, though it got me back writing seriously again.

The whole Eamon/Frankee retaliation thing from 2004 got me thinking. Frankee had released a fight-back single to put her side of the story after Eamon's version of their break-up had topped the charts. I wrote a response for anything Charlotte might write about me – maybe one day I'll give it to someone else and see how they get on with it.

About a year after splitting with Charlotte I felt I'd got my life back on course. I had decided to focus on music production. There's so much talent in Cardiff and South Wales and I wanted to help some of it develop and get the recognition it deserved. My business partner and I, Marcus Simpson, have got a studio – X'Plicit Music – fully up and running, and we are building a catalogue of artists to work with.

We sorted out and shot a great video for the 13-year-old rapper Jenna Louise Dickens who is known as JLD. Marcus and I wrote the script and when we had it approved I got on the phone to everyone from Jenna's school to a local car showroom to get permission to film on their premises. We had a whole American flavour to it, with some other scenes shot in a local diner, and it was a brilliant experience. We're also working with a group, Spotlight, who made it through to the fourth round of *The X Factor* and we're also talking to Bristol-based singer-songwriter Rosie. It's a steep learning curve for all of us, and it's taking a lot of our time. But we're hoping it will all pay off in the end.

In all of this, being behind the scenes really suits me and I didn't care how many hours I spent at the studio, trying to get the best out of people. It is where I feel at home and where I feel like a professional.

Talking of home, my dad's street in Cardiff is even closer to all the good new stuff, now that the massive Wales Millennium Centre has been built just a few hundred metres away. Charlotte sang there on its big opening night and my dad, my neighbours and I weren't just over the moon that Maria Church was still bad-mouthing us. The *People* newspaper carried a big story saying Charlotte was terrified of being kidnapped by gangs who thought they could get a share of her fortune. 'These are worrying times. We've had our fair share of death threats and stalkers,' said Maria before really putting the knife in. 'It was more of a worry when she was seeing Steven because of the area he lives in. It's a really rough part of the city. We heard rumours of a kidnapping.'

Thanks, Maria. We know you had trouble selling your house when Charlotte moved out. But that doesn't mean you have to make it so hard for our neighbours to sell theirs. Anyway, time has passed and I'm not letting that stuff get to me any more, though I can't say for sure that everyone else on the street feels the same.

Amazingly enough, other jobs do still occasionally come up and I hope I am finally winning them in my own right rather than off the back of anyone else. For example, in 2004 I got a call out of the blue that Channel Four were doing a new celebrity dating show – and they wanted me to take part. At first, as usual, I thought it was probably a wind-up. I'm not exactly a celebrity and, as I've never gone in for trying to get seen at premieres and parties, I was convinced it was a mate trying to make a fool out of me. Or, worse, maybe it was a reporter making up the whole idea to do some story about how I think I'm a celebrity – and if I agree to go on the fictional show they'll do some awful story about me. One thing I've learned since meeting Charlotte is that in her world you can never automatically trust anyone again.

Anyway I found out that the show really was genuine. They wanted to put a group of guys and girls in a flat in London together, take them out and film them on dates and get their verdicts on who was the most romantic. It sounded like a lot of fun. At that point I was single, and the women the producers thought they were going to get for the show sounded fantastic. I couldn't see any reason to turn the show down.

The producers did end up getting a great group of people together for the show – the women were Judi Shekoni from *EastEnders*, models Donatello and Lauren

Pope and Aimee from *Popstars: The Rivals*. Alongside me in the guys corner were Ray from *Big Brother 4*, Paris from *Fame Academy 2* and Vassos from *The Salon*. It was a two-week job and I was nervous about meeting everybody, but it turned out to be a laugh from the start. What made it even better was being able to turn people's expectations on their heads. 'We thought you'd be a real tosser. None of us thought we'd even want to talk to you,' they said one night when we were well into the show.

'Everyone thinks that. They always do, probably always will,' I replied. Interestingly enough I got a brilliant way to prove to these people that almost everything the papers said about me was a lie. One of the people who was supposed to have been on the show, going on her first date with me, was Abi Titmuss. One paper said we had hit it off so well that we were secretly dating behind the producers' backs. But Abi had pulled out of the show before filming had even begun. We had never even met, let alone done any of the things the newspapers claimed.

Back on the show, my best date was with Aimee and getting to go to Paris on Eurostar was a blast as well. The camera crew were relaxed and, while I don't normally like being interviewed on camera, they made it all feel easy. I didn't win the show or even come close. But the whole thing was a bit of a laugh, which was a pleasant change, and I hopefully made some new friends out of it.

Just before the dating show I'd had one call from one of the weekly women's magazines to do a big fashion shoot. We had a couple of nights in London, they also did a big interview on my career and my future and I met some cool models from Storm. It was good fun, and the cheque I got, added to the ones from the dating show and other bits of other work, helped me get my finances sorted. I was still happy living in the top-floor room at my dad's house, but I wanted to own a place of my own so I used some of the cash to put a deposit on a place in town. The rest went on a car and new kit for my recording studio. I really felt like I felt I was surviving on my own and putting down some real foundations for the future. From now on I could focus on making music.

What I couldn't ever do was escape the past. One day in the spring of 2005 I got a call from my sister to say that I was in *OK!* magazine again. She brought it round and it was a big piece all about Charlotte's new boyfriend, but it included loads of stuff and pictures about me. It's bizarre to have it all brought back like this, without having any warning. But I suppose with many of these articles, which seem like a rewrite of old quotes and rumours, even Charlotte wouldn't know that they were appearing. Neither, of course, would her boyfriend Gavin Henson.

No one in my family could really believe it when we first heard on the Cardiff grapevine that Charlotte was seeing Gavin. He was pretty famous for his hairstyles and his flash boots, but even so he was supposed to be so focused on rugby that you only ever expected to read about him on the sports pages, not the gossip columns.

Charlotte was now a full-time fixture on the gossip pages, however. Some of her coverage was funny – as when the press got a picture of her on the beach looking like she had piled on the pounds during a holiday in Ibiza with her mates. Back in Britain her mum was quoted saying she had put on too much weight for a photo-shoot and was on a crash diet to get ready to do the shots in a few weeks. WHO ATE ALL THE PIE JESUS, CHARLOTTE? was the headline on one paper's story, which you have to admit is pretty good.

Charlotte wasn't just eating a lot at this point, however. Her boozy nights out were becoming legendary, in Cardiff and beyond. My mates and I tried to avoid the kind of places she was likely to be at, though often the mobile would ring to tell us her gang was heading in a certain direction so we could change our plans if we wanted. But even if we didn't see her in person, we would see the pictures in the papers over the next few days. We also heard the stories of the police being called to Charlotte's home several times when neighbours could no longer put up with the music and the partying.

Charlotte's London nights out seemed even bigger – and got even more publicity. One of the first big nights was on her 18th birthday when she yelled out, 'I'm 18 and I'll drink if I want to,' after all the problems she had had as the world's most famous 16- and 17-year-old wannabe boozer. She, the girls and Kyle, had been at Boujis in South Kensington knocking back champagne, vodka and her favourite cranberry cocktails. Coming out of the club at 1.30am, before heading on to Trap, she fell flat on her backside in the street, right in front of the photographers – CHARLOTTE LURCH the headline writers came up with the next day. Another time, when climbing into her car after another boozy night out, she realised too late that her dress was a bit too loose and flimsy up top to cover her up.

Sometimes the reporting was at least tongue-in-cheek. 'Today promises to be a momentous occasion for the Welsh nation. There is a possibility – slim, admittedly – that Charlotte Church will wake up without a hangover,' wrote the *Daily Mail* under the headline, HE PLAYS RUGBY FOR WALES. SHE DRINKS FOR WALES.

'Earlier this week Charlotte promised to stay in last night – a sacrifice never known to have been made before – to rest her voice ahead of her big TV date when millions of viewers and a crowd of 73,000 will watch Charlotte sing the Welsh National Anthem live on the pitch of Cardiff's Millennium Stadium, where Wales are to meet Ireland for the climax of the Six Nations rugby championship,' said the reporter.

For so long I had been the bad boy in Charlotte's life, but now suddenly she was the bad girl, all on her own.

The papers started to put Charlotte in the mould they had made for me. Instead of me supposedly leeching off and dragging down my perfect girlfriend, she was accused of doing exactly the same with her squeaky-clean boyfriend.

'The pair are getting in as much quality time as they can before spiky-haired Gavin jets off to New Zealand for the Lions tour at the end of the month. Well, someone has to pay the bills,' jibed the *Mirror* in one example of this new trend. And it was only the beginning…

'On the face of it, Gavin and Charlotte do not share the same aspirations and ideals,' wrote a different reporter. 'Henson's whole life is devoted to rugby and he is a fitness fanatic. He allows himself just one night out a week and seldom drinks anything but alcopops. In contrast, Charlotte's favourite pastime is getting completely plastered. To take just one example, the former child prodigy's 19th birthday party a couple of weeks ago lasted 72 hours. Her favourite tipple is vodka and Red Bull, plus white wine, champagne and rum cocktails. And so when rumours began circulating that the pair were romatically linked, Henson was strongly advised by his people "not to get involved with her" – advice he appears to have ignored.'

The criticism didn't stop there. 'Gavin is the rising star of Welsh rugby and there are hopes he will become the next Jonny Wilkinson,' a so-called 'rugby source' was quoted as saying in the *Daily Mail*. 'So there is a feeling that the last thing he needs is a girlfriend who spends her time going out getting completely wrecked. She is bound to try and persuade him to go out with her on her wild binges and that's the very last thing he needs.'

The paper then went on to rehash all the coverage of Charlotte's 19th birthday bender. 'This, then, is what Gavin Henson is up against,' it concluded. 'It won't be easy for someone who says he hasn't got the energy to go out more than once a week. So will Charlotte change all that, or will Henson be the one to tame her? Friends believe that at present Charlotte is untameable. "She's utterly wild, completely out of control," says a source. "It's hard to envisage Charlotte staying in on a Saturday night with a DVD and a takeaway. She will want to take Gavin out partying with her and the question is whether he will be strong enough to resist." No doubt if Wales triumph today Charlotte has plans for as wild a bender as even her 19th birthday. Today Henson will need all his reserves of energy and fighting spirit. And that's just off the pitch.'

Oddly enough, when Charlotte and I were together we did, in fact, spend loads of Saturday nights in with a DVD and a takeaway – it was one of our favourite things and it's still one of mine. But even allowing for all the usual distortions in the press, it's clear that Charlotte does seem to be partying harder than ever. Obviously she and I went out a lot together when we were dating. But we hardly ever got drunk.

I sometimes wondered if there was some sort of child-star syndrome going on with Charlotte. By that I mean that child stars, taken away from an ordinary school and home life and made to work long hours surrounded by adults, will ultimately rebel and try to create the childhood they feel they have never had.

Charlotte, from the first time I ever spoke to her, was desperate to prove she was just one of the girls, that there was no difference between her life and that of her mates. She was also desperate to lose the angelic image that had been built up for so long, so if someone in the gang had one drink, she had to have two. But even so, the Charlotte I knew then still knew her limits. A lot of what she did was pushing the line to have an effect, but she also had a sense of where to stop.

One friend reckons Charlotte has always just wanted to rebel against her parents – even when she doesn't know she's doing it. She got that job done by going out with me, knowing full well that they would never like me. Now she's going out with someone they do approve of, she's got to find another way to get under their skin. Which is by drinking, behaving badly and making them worry that she'll never work hard at anything again.

The other thing Charlotte had when we were together was a focus. We talked about music every day and spent a lot of time in my home and work studios, knocking ideas and sounds around. I knew she had recorded other tracks, so I was puzzled about the long delay in releasing her first non-classical album. When we were together she was in so many studios with different producers, writers and musicians – everyone from Take That star Gary Barlow to Robbie Williams' former writing partner Guy Chambers and R&B star Fitzgerald Scott. I'd heard a lot of the work she had done and thought it was great. So, like everyone else, I was waiting for the album in the summer of 2004. Then in the autumn of 2004. Then in the early months of 2005...

All through all this time rumours were circulating about arguments over the album's style and direction, and whether or not Charlotte was working on replacement tracks. When Charlotte had a big hit with 'Crazy Chick' in the summer of 2005 and the album finally saw the light of day, I reckon that's the best thing that could have happened for her. Because the Charlotte I knew wasn't ever a drifter, she was a grafter. She might like to pretend she just wanted to have a big family and loads of dogs, as she told the papers at the end of 2004. But in reality she wanted to keep on climbing mountains. That's why she was in talks to star in a film before she had even done her GCSEs.

When we were dating, Charlotte was happiest in two different situations. The first was when we were alone together in our home, listening to music, watching TV, lazing in bed or lying back in the bath looking at the stars through the skylight. Secondly she was happy when she was performing, either in concert or at any other event where she was in the spotlight and I was in the wings or a step behind holding her hand for support.

The situations she didn't like so much were when I was out with others, or when the cameras were on me at a modelling shoot. That means it's always going to be very hard for any of Charlotte's boyfriends to know just what their role should be. I felt I was making her miserable and insecure when I went out to try and get some work and make a serious career for myself. Instead there was always pressure on me to stay at home and spend the day in bed whenever she had free time. But Kyle found that wasting days in bed and being on hand 24/7 didn't work, either. One of the reasons Charlotte gave for that relationship ending was that she felt he wasn't doing enough to build a life and an income of his own. Work that one out!

Will any man be allowed to find a middle ground? Gavin Henson has given it a go. No one can accuse him of not having drive and ambition, and his fame and fortune is to be found on a rugby pitch surrounded by other men, which is a lot less threatening than being with beautiful models. Charlotte has to decide whether she is ready to share her limelight.

I admire Charlotte for sticking to Wales and to her old mates. I reckon she still has a great career ahead of her – if that's the way she wants to go. I just hope that one way or the other she finds a way to do it on her own terms, without any pressures from the people who make money out of her. I hope she ends up happy.

And, as for me, writing this book closes a chapter on my life. Too many lies have been written about me, my family and my time with Charlotte. I needed to put my side of the story out there. I needed to explain who Steve Johnson really is, and how different he is from the picture that has been painted in all the papers. I'm nowhere near perfect, and I don't always act the hero. And in the manic world of sudden celebrity I know I made mistakes in a whole lot of things.

One thing I don't regret, though, is ever asking Charlotte for a kiss that first night when she and her mates came round to my dad's house to listen to some music. The time we had together wasn't always happy, but I don't regret any of that either. I want to see Charlotte go on to good things. She has got a great voice, a big talent, and if she wants to be a top international star again then I hope she makes it. But if she really wants to throw it all in and become a perfect wife and mother, then I hope that works out as well.

Either way, one day I hope we can meet each other on equal terms and thank each other for being there when our lives were out of our control and we had to just hold on to each other to get through the day.

The key thing I have learned is that ordinary guys don't always survive in the megastar world. We don't fit alongside all the minders, the media and the millions that come with real celebrity. We live in a different world and we have different dreams. We don't mix with legends or speak to reporters. Instead we meet nice local girls, maybe teachers, nurses, receptionists. We fall in love and we try and build a good life with a strong family. That's the life my parents have always had. It's the life I always saw for myself before I met Charlotte. And that's the life I want to find today.